How to Grow

RARE GREENHOUSE PLANTS

Author of *Greenhouse Gardening for Everyone*

How To Grow RARE GREENHOUSE PLANTS

260 Flowering Varieties

for Amateur and Florist

by ERNEST CHABOT

GRAMERCY PUBLISHING COMPANY

Library of Congress Catalog Card Number: 74-77814

This edition is published by Gramercy Publishing Company
a division of Crown Publishers, Inc.
by arrangement with M. Barrows & Company, Inc.
c d e f g h
Manufactured in the United States of America

Contents

Illustrations

All photographs by Jack Roche except Clerodendron, Haemanthus, and Vallota by author.

In Appreciation

No sooner was *Greenhouse Gardening For Everyone* completed than many experienced plantsmen began to call my attention to the numerous, fine greenhouse plants omitted from that book. Amateur that I am, I realized that most of them were unfamiliar to me. Encouragement came from all directions, however, and little by little I began to try the "new" things suggested by these enthusiasts. Their inspiration, backed by constructive help and patience with my inexperience, made this book possible.

To E. J. Alexander of the New York Botanical Garden, I am especially indebted for his untiring assistance in the selection of the plant material and with the nomenclature. He is a wizard at plant identification. Many dealers in unusual plant material were of great help, and gave freely of their vast experience in cultural practices, especially Cecil Houdyshel of La Verne, California; Wyndham Hayward of Winter Park, Florida; Mulford B. Foster of Orlando, Florida; Rex D. Pearce of Moorestown, New Jersey; J. N. Giridlian of Oakhurst Gardens, Arcadia, California; and Julius Roehrs of Rutherford, New Jersey.

For help with the chapter on pests and diseases, I am most

grateful to that great team of the New York State College of Agriculture at Cornell University—Dr. A. W. Dimock and Dr. W. E. Blauvelt.

There are many others to whom I owe a real debt of gratitude for furnishing data, checking portions of the manuscript and tolerating endless questions and correspondence—Patrick J. McKenna, garden writer and consultant horticulturist of New York City; John Swan, Pat Connelly, and Walter Singer of the New York Botanical Garden; Theodore A. Weston, editor of *Flower Grower;* Paul Frese, editor of *Popular Gardening;* Helen Van Pelt Wilson, author of many popular garden books; Lord & Burnham, greenhouse manufacturers; Dr. Harold E. Anthony of Englewood, New Jersey, Professor Alex Laurie and Dr. D. C. Kiplinger of Ohio State University, Victor Greiff of Neponsit, New York, Dr. Kenneth Post of Cornell University, and Professor Paul Krone of Michigan State College.

Another whom I wish to thank is my secretary, Irene Baranowski, for endless research, attention to detail, correspondence, typing, retyping and retyping. Without her energetic and untiring help, this work would have been several more years in the doing.

Tarrytown, New York ERNEST CHABOT

1

The Fascination of Growing Unfamiliar Flowers

It is a rare adventure to bring into bloom plants you never saw before, to have flowers not usually seen in florists' shops or displayed at shows. There is Haemanthus Katharinae with blood-red, sphere-shaped blossoms—the immense, silver-gray flower of Iris Susiana marked with deep purple veins—Columnea gloriosa's tubular, scarlet-yellow flowers appearing from beautiful velvety leaves—Lotus Berthelotii with brilliant red, pea-shaped blossoms and drooping silvery foliage. These flowers are so altogether striking they seem unreal. To grow them in your own greenhouse brings a kind of pleasure to be had in no other way.

At our home, the genuine fascination of such unusual plants is shown by the large number of visitors who come to see them again and again. The wonder and pleasure of friends in the rare flowers they have never seen before is one of our just delights. We have a standing joke, however, that goes with this natural pride. On an evening when company is expected, we bring a few choice plants into the house for decoration, but just as soon as the company leaves, the plants go back to the greenhouse while they are still fresh and lovely.

You, too, can have the pleasures of growing these unfamiliar flowering plants that include some of the most beautiful in the world. Many bloom over an exceptionally long period. With careful selection, you can have a gorgeous show throughout most of the year—something out of the ordinary in flower at all times. Most of us are inclined to think of the winter garden too much in terms of the florist's familiar garden annuals. Not that there is anything wrong with them. In fact, as I pointed out in *Greenhouse Gardening For Everyone,* these annuals are excellent for a quick splash of color, especially if they are planted for a succession of bloom. But many of us do not have time to keep them coming along in the small greenhouse. We need, and must have, material of a more permanent character, plants we can count on continuously to give color and excitement to a year-round program.

Such are the plants described in this book. All are flowering, and self-perpetuating by cuttings, division of root stock, or offsets. All can be successfully grown in pots, and many will do well for years without shifting or transplanting. Of course, this handbook of rare flowering greenhouse plants is by no means complete, but representative of the most suitable types and vast possibilities. Some excellent plants have been omitted because I could not find a ready source of supply for them. (See list on pages 16 to 18.) There are hundreds of other plants well worth seeking out, to say nothing of the sub-varieties and hybrids of those which have been described. You never finish following their trails, and can go on and on experimenting in this unlimited field.

If you are a beginner just starting out with a new greenhouse, don't let the long, tongue-twisting Latin names keep you from growing these plants. The fact is, you'll soon be using these names yourself. Familiarity with names comes readily with familiarity with plants. Established specimens of almost all of these plants are comparatively easy to grow, much easier and less exacting, in fact, than many of the annuals. It is mostly a question of supplying the right environment. And these plants are a challenge, too. They offer a long series of surprises and pleasures to all who enjoy working in a greenhouse.

Of course, it is not possible to grow all of these plants in one greenhouse. You have to select kinds that require similar conditions of temperature, light, and humidity. There are cool-house, warm-house, and moderate temperature plants here, and many of considerable adaptability. Except in a few cases, where type plants are used to describe others in a genera and more detailed information is wanted, I have not considered plants covered in my first book. Orchids are not included, since there are so many excellent books devoted to them exclusively.

This book is devoted to flowering plants alone, mainly unusual ones. The management of a greenhouse and the growing of the more familiar plants is covered in detail in *Greenhouse Gardening For Everyone*. I include here, however, some information on pests and diseases (pages 19-25), and this word about fertilizers:

When ammonium sulphate or nitrate of soda is recommended, it is assumed that superphosphate or a complete fertilizer, such as a 4-10-4 or 5-10-5, has been added to the soil beforehand, as explained in the first book. Ammonium sulphate and nitrate of soda are among the best and least expensive carriers of nitrogen, but they are not *complete* fertilizers. Phosphorous is best added before planting—a 4-inch potful to a bushel of soil. Phosphorus moves slowly and takes time to become available as plant food. Ammonium sulphate that has an acid reaction is used in locations where soil tends to be alkaline, or with plants that need an acid soil, such as Ismenes, Crinums, and Lycoris. Nitrate of soda, on the other hand, is alkaline and should be used with soils that are acid or for plants requiring less acidity, such as Cytisus, Arthropodium, and Gazanias. When phosphorus has not been previously added, a complete fertilizer should be used. It is simply to clarify the practices of greenhouse fertilizing to those who may not have read my first book, that this is mentioned here.

GROW THESE FOR FRAGRANCE

The fascination of unfamiliar flowers is not confined to their unique form and coloring alone. Coupled with this enjoyment is the exciting fragrance of many of the blossoms. Even a group of these plants chosen at random is likely to include a few that would give a touch of natural fragrance, but selections from the list that follows will insure it:

Albuca
Boronia
Brunfelsia (Franciscea)—
  Lady-Of-The-Night
Brunsvigia
Cestrum duirnum, nocturnum
  & Parqui
Choisya ternata—Mexican
  Orange Flower
Clerodendron fragrans—
  Glory Bower or Tree
Crinum and Amarcrinum
Daphne odora
Eucharis—Amazon Lily
Gladiolus tristis and blandus
Hoya carnosa—Wax Plant
Ismene (Hymenocallis)—
  Sea Daffodil or Spider Lily
Ixora parviflora
Jasminum
Leucocoryne—Glory-of-the-Sun
Luculia

Milla biflora
Ornithogalum
Rochea coccinea
Stephanotis floribunda–
Madagascar Jasmine
Tabernaemontana
Trachelospermum jasminoides
(Rhynchospermum)–Star or
Confederate Jasmine
Tulbaghia fragrans
Watsonia marginata

Liberty Hyde Bailey's *Hortus Second* has been my guide and authority for plant names. In a few cases, I give synonyms or almost obsolete names in parenthesis because these are sometimes used in catalogs.

Recommended night temperatures by artificial heat are given for each plant. Daytime temperatures by the sun's heat may be safely run at least 10°F. higher.

2

Where to Find Rare Plants

Discovering sources of unusual plants to grow in your greenhouse can be a lot of fun. Most of the less common kinds of seeds, bulbs, and plants are grown by specialists, and while their catalogs and lists are not as colorful as those of the larger seed houses, their enthusiasm is catching. Before you know it, you will be making up a long list of "must haves." You will find the plantsmen themselves most cooperative, too, and correspondence with them educational and pleasant.

The plants covered in this book are not available from any one source, or from the same source at all times. Some of the items are rare and stocks run out. With persistence, though, you will be able to locate what you want.

Always buy the very best stock you can for greenhouse gardening. You have a big investment in the greenhouse and want good results. Seed that is not viable, bulbs that are diseased or are not yet of flowering size, and plants that are infected or poorly rooted can only bring disappointment. The best material may sometimes seem expensive, but it will yield choice blooms that are worth much more than money. I have found that it pays to order top-sized bulbs and young plants rather than to try to grow everything from seed. What is wanted is a good show with plenty of flowers. Of course, some subjects are only available from seed, and a deep fondness for plants you raise yourself is only natural, but it is not wise to try too many kinds from seed at one time. They can become a burden. Some seedlings, however, along with mature plants give a lot of satisfaction.

Many of my friends who are home greenhouse gardeners like to buy from foreign countries, where there are sources for varieties not available here. Seedsmen in South Africa, England, India, Holland, Belgium, Germany, France, Switzerland, Canada, Hawaii, South America, and Mexico carry a wide assortment of rare plants, and you may want to try some which they offer. Seed can come into this country without inspection, but quarantine regulations designed to protect us from various infestations require that bulbs and plants be admitted only through the Bureau of Entomology and Plant Quarantine. Plants frequently do not come through too well, for in addition to a long trip, they may also have to endure fumigation, which can add to their setback.

To import bulbs or plants, write to the Import and Permit Section office located nearest to you, and request a form which must be filled out to accompany your foreign orders. You can get this information from offices in the following cities: Mobile, Alabama; Douglas, Arizona; San Francisco, California; Miami, Florida; Savannah, Georgia; Chicago, Illinois; New Orleans, Louisiana; Baltimore, Maryland; Boston, Massachusetts; Detroit, Michigan; St. Paul, Minnesota; St. Louis, Missouri; Buffalo, New York; Hoboken, New Jersey; Cleveland, Ohio; Portland, Oregon; Philadelphia, Pennsylvania; Charleston, South Carolina; Laredo, Texas; Norfolk, Virginia; Seattle, Washington.

The following sources of supplies are by no means complete, but according to *The Plant Buyer's Guide* and my own extensive catalog file, all the plant material described in this book can be obtained through one source or another. If you are looking for something not listed in a catalog, write anyway to the most likely supplier. Perhaps he has it, but in too small an amount to catalog; if he does not have it, he may be able to suggest someone who does. Also, write to your local botanical garden, agricultural college, or experiment station. They can often help you find what you want of these rare and lovely plants.

SOURCES OF SUPPLY

Armstrong Nurseries
Ontario, Calif.

S. S. Berry
Redlands, Calif.

Burgess Seed & Plant Co.
Galesburg, Mich.

Cactus Pete
5440 Valley Blvd.
Los Angeles 32, Calif.

California Nursery Co.
Niles, Calif.

Carroll Gardens
Westminster, Md.

Chatauqua Flowerfield Co.
Greenhurst, N. Y.

Coolidge Rare Plant Gardens
889 N. Foothill Blvd.
Pasadena, Calif.

Evans & Reeves
255 S. Barrington Ave.
W. Los Angeles, Calif.

Exotic Gardens
2790 N.W. 17th Ave.
Miami, Fla.

Fantastic Gardens
R. G. Wilson
Rt. 2, Box 2324
So. Miami 43, Fla.

Florida Nursery & Landscape Co.
Leesburg, Fla.

Mulford B. Foster
718 Magnolia Ave.
Orlando, Fla.

Fruitland Nurseries
Augusta, Ga.

Germain's
Los Angeles, Calif.

Glen St. Mary Nursery
Glen St. Mary, Fla.

Griffing Nurseries
P. O. Box 3389
Beaumont, Tex.

Hallawell Seed and
Nursery Co.
519 Market Street
San Francisco 5, Calif.

Hav'alook Gardens
10045 W. Grand River Ave.
Fowlerville, Mich.

Wyndham Hayward
Winter Park, Fla.

Holmes Nurseries
P.O. Box 417
Tampa 1, Fla.

Cecil E. Houdyshel
1412 E. Third St.
Laverne, Calif.

Paul J. Howard's Flowerland
11700 National Blvd.
Los Angeles, Calif.

Hughes Seed Store
116 S. Miami Ave.
Miami 1, Fla.

Island Landscape Co.
Box 110
Palm Beach, Fla.

La Rochette Nursery
1195 Stanyan Street
San Francisco 17, Calif.

E. A. Martin Seed Co.
202 E. Bay Street
Jacksonville, Fla.

L. B. Merrick Nurseries
9531 E. Whittier Blvd.
Pico, Calif.

Mitchell Nurseries, Inc.
Barre, Vt.

North Street Greenhouses
57 North Street
Danielson, Conn.

J. N. Giridlian
Oakhurst Gardens
345 W. Colorado St.
Arcadia, Calif.

Rex D. Pearce
Moorestown, N. J.

Portland Camellia Nursery
3307 No. Williams Ave.
Portland 12, Ore.

Carl Purdy Gardens
Ukiah, Calif.

Julius Roehrs
Rutherford, N. J.

Royal Palm Nurseries
Oneco, Fla.

Saxton & Wilson
Maplewood, Ore.

Select Nurseries
1200 W. Whittier Blvd.
Whittier, Calif.

Shaffer Nurseries
North Highland Ave.
Clearwater, Fla.

The Barnes Importers
East Aurora 2, N. Y.

Wayside Gardens
Mentor, Ohio

C. R. Worth
Groton, N. Y.

3

Pests and Diseases

Modern insecticides make it simple to keep your greenhouse free of practically all insects. Two or three sure controls, even for those hard-to-kill insects like mealy bug, white fly, and red spider are now available to us. Unfortunately, these marvelous new bug killers are very strong poisons, only to be used with precaution. With common sense care, however, no home greenhouse gardener should be harmed by them.

PEST CONTROL

Here is a system some of my friends and I follow. We use this spray about once every two weeks in the summer, from May to September, and once every three weeks the rest of the year:

To 1 gallon water, add:
1 level tablespoon parathion 15 percent wettable powder (Poison)
1 level tablespoon Fermate
1 level tablespoon wettable sulphur, when needed
1 level teaspoon Dreft, as spreader

The spray is of mild concentration, as should be, so as not to harm tender plants. Applications every two or three weeks are necessary to protect new growth as it develops.

The parathion gets red spider mite, mealy bug, white fly, green fly, aphids, thrips, scale, midge and leaf hopper, tier, miner, roller, and such. The residue on the foliage from one spraying continues to kill for a week or more.

Fermate is a fungicide that helps keep botrytis, septorial leaf spot, and rust in check. Parzate or Karbam may be used in place of Fermate if you prefer. Wettable sulphur controls mildew and may be added for plants that are susceptible to it.

Parathion with Precautions. Parathion is a strong organic poison! It must be used with respect, especially within the confines of a small greenhouse. But this is true of many of the other insecticides we might use, such as nicotine sulphate, Cyanogas, and others that are not nearly as effective.

Wear a Good Respirator. It sounds and looks like a lot of trouble, fuss and bother, but there's nothing to it, and the job doesn't take long. The respirator, a small affair that fits over your nose and mouth, should be of the chemical cartridge type such as the Agrisol Respirator made by the Willson Company of Reading, or the Parathion Farm Respirator made by the Mines Safety Appliance Co., of Pittsburgh, both in Pennsylvania. They are not expensive and are available through the larger seed houses. A complete gas mask such as florists use with the parathion aerosol bomb is not necessary. In fact, those aerosols require too many precautions for the amateur and are better left alone.

This Is Important. Wear the respirator when measuring the powder as well as when spraying.

Handle the parathion powder with care when putting it in the sprayer.

Avoid inhaling the fumes or raising a dust.

Leave the ventilators open when you spray and after spraying. Give the vapor an hour or more to settle before entering again. If you have a greenhouse joined to your home, keep the door leading into the house closed.

Finally, immediately after spraying, wash all exposed skin surfaces—hands, arms, and face.

An Effective Fumigant. If your greenhouse is not joined to your home, fumigation is easier than spraying and nearly as effective. It is also safer since you are not exposed to the poisonous vapors. Among those available are the Parathion Fumigator made by the Fuller Systems, Incorporated, of Woburn, Massachusetts, and the Plantfume 103 Smoke Generator (containing dithio) of the Plant Products Corporation at Blue Point, Long Island, New York.

The Parathion Fumigator comes in sizes for 1000 and 2000 cubic feet, but for smaller greenhouses, the required proportion of the contents may be burned in a small container such as an empty frozen fruit juice can. More frequent treatment may be required with fumigation than spray, since the residual kill for hatching larvae is lacking.

The Plantfume 103 Smoke Generator is similar. At present, it is only put up in containers for 1000 and 5000 cubic feet. These cannot be broken down for smaller greenhouses, but if there is sufficient demand, the manufacturer tells me he will make units of other sizes.

Remember to close all ventilators tightly before treatment. If you have automatic ventilation, set the thermostat up high or switch off the electric current so the sash will not open. Fumigation may be done day or night if the foliage is dry and if the temperature will not go beyond 90°F. with ventilators closed. A temperature of 70° to 75° is satisfactory.

Sparklers are supplied to ignite the contents. Light the sparkler from the bottom or handle end, insert the top in the fumigator, and get out of the greenhouse. The gas comes off slowly at first and later completely fills the house. It's all over for the pests in about eight hours. Then the ventilators should be opened.

I have used both these fumigators, without any ill effect, in my own greenhouse when it contained a wide variety of plants, including many tender tropicals. Of course, all open flowers were picked beforehand.

Other Insecticides. It goes without saying that if you are at all wary of parathion, you should not consider it for one moment. There are many good, less poisonous, and safer insecticides you can use. It is not necessary to have a large assortment for the home greenhouse, either; just two or three should be enough for a complete job.

Rotenone sprays and dusts, available under many brand names, are excellent for the control of a large number of insects and preferable to nicotine sulphate and pyrethrum sprays. They will get red spider mite, aphids, green fly, thrips, and many other insects. Most can be used in combination with DDT. According to tests by Bill Blauvelt of Cornell University, NNOR Garden Spray and Wilson's Spi-Tox have been among the most satisfactory. The new Tri-ogen No. 2 formula is of this type. Rototec Garden Spray of the Plant Products Corporation is one of the most effective rotenone sprays against mites. Protexall and Jackson and Perkins' Rose Spray have been reasonably effective. Rotenone dusts have not been satisfactory for mite control. Apomite, still another fine rotenone spray of the Liberty Chemical Laboratories of Maywood, Illinois, is effective against red spider, thrips, aphids, green fly, white fly and other insects.

Dimite, available at Sherwin-Williams paint stores and Aramite 15-W made by the U. S. Rubber Company at Bethany, Connecticut, are very effective on red spider mite, but have little or no effect on insects. They are relatively non-poisonous to man.

DDT will get scale, midge, thrips, leaf tier, some species of leaf rollers, and many other pests, against which it is far superior to arsenate of lead. It is also effective against white fly, though it only kills the adult fly and must be used about once a week. Rotenone and nicotine sulphate may be mixed with DDT to kill the suckling insects. Dusting in the walks and under the benches occasionally with DDT will keep slugs, sow bugs, and snails in check. Like parathion, it is particularly good because the residue on the foliage continues to give protection for weeks after application. Use a 50 percent DDT wettable powder at 1 level tablespoonful to 1 gallon of water, or a safe type of 25 percent DDT emulsion such as Detex formulated for use on horticultural plants.

Buggeta pellets, containing metaldehyde as a potent "lure," are effective in killing slugs and snails. Simply toss a few pellets under the benches, or place one or two on the soil surface.

Thrips, which rasp the foliage and leave it yellow and half dead, can be controlled now with Isotox Garden Spray (containing lindane) used at seven to ten day intervals. It leaves an invisible residue which kills thrips as well as aphids, white fly, leaf hoppers, and many other major insect pests.

DISEASES

Diseases are more easily avoided than controlled—healthful growing practices being more effective than sprays or dusts. Cleanliness, good air circulation, plenty of light, and even temperatures, the essential requisites, are easy to provide in a tight, well-designed greenhouse equipped with ample ventilation and a good heating system. Drafts, sudden drops in temperature, dripping water from condensation, and musty conditions are always to be avoided.

On very cold days when heat is on most of the time, there is a good circulation of air. In warm weather, you can open the ventilators to keep the air fresh. It is those dull, muggy days and nights of fall and spring that can cause trouble. Leaving the roof ventilators open an inch or two at night, and maintaining temperature and air circulation by burning a little more fuel, keeps the greenhouse fresh and "right."

Do not run a hospital for sick plants. Be ruthless in discarding any that are infested. Diseases spread easily from one plant to another.

Pick off and throw out dead or diseased foliage and blooms. Never permit rubbish to accumulate under the benches or anywhere else in the greenhouse.

Inspect all new plants before bringing them into your greenhouse. Do not give diseased plants house room. Also, take the precaution of spraying or fumigating them for insects before adding them to your collection.

Splashing water spreads disease. Water with care and in the mornings on bright days when possible with the ventilators open. Condensation on the foliage at night is sure to breed fungi and bacteria.

Insects spread disease. Have a systematic schedule of pest control and stick to it.

Use sterilized soil, if possible.

DISEASE CONTROL

One or two fungicidal sprays or dusts are essential in the greenhouse.

Fermate gives good control of botrytis and other diseases on most plants. It may be used as a spray or dust and can be mixed with most insecticides. It is also excellent for treating cuttings to be propagated.

Ortho 406 or Wilson's Anti-Damp are recent developments that give remarkable control for damping-off as well as many diseases.

Wettable sulphur is effective against mildew and may be mixed with DDT for control of the disease and chewing insects as well.

There are several name-brand all-purpose fungicides on the market that may be used in place of sulphur. One is Botano de Luxe, containing fermate, methoxyclor, and several other ingredients.

Great progress is being made every year in insect and disease control. The best controls that can be recommended today may be replaced by new ones tomorrow. Right now, in fact, a new insecticide is in the trial stages that nearly parallels parathion in effectiveness yet is safe enough to use without special precautions. Watch for such new developments that are always under way. Perhaps in time we will have a perfect insecticide and fungicide, all in one, as effective as parathion, yet safe enough for a baby to handle.

4

Terms to Know

ANTHER. The sac or top part of the stamen that carries the pollen.

AXIL. The angle formed by a leaf or flower stalk with the stem.

BELL JAR OR GLASS. A bell-shaped glass used to cover cuttings or seed plantings that need a higher temperature and close moist atmosphere.

BLINDNESS. Failure to produce blooms.

BRACT. A leaf associated with the flowers. It may or may not have a flower stem.

CHLOROSIS. Deficiency of chlorophyll or green coloring matter in a plant. Symptoms are yellowing or whitening of the foliage and stems.

CLOSED CASE. A box covered with glass in which cuttings are rooted and seed is germinated. Usually a section of greenhouse bench 8 inches deep with a glazed sash hinged at the back to raise the temperature and increase the humidity. Additional heat is furnished by electric soil heating cable.

CORM. A solid, enlarged, underground stem. Roots are produced from its lower surface; leaves and buds from the upper.

CYME. Broad, flat-topped, usually branched flower cluster in which the center flowers blossom first.

DAMP-OFF. Fungus diseases that occur at the stem of a seedling where it emerges from the soil. It is usually sure death to the plant.

HEAD. A dense cylindrical, or spherical flower cluster at the end of a stem.

HERBACEOUS. Not having a firm woody structure. Lacking persistent stems above ground.

INFLORESCENCE. Flower forms. The arrangement of the flowers on a plant.

LAYERING. A method of propagating plants by causing roots to form on stems that are still a part of the plant.

MEDIUM. The material used to germinate seed or root cuttings such as sand, soil, peatmoss, or vermiculite.

MIDRIB. The main rib of a leaf. A continuation of the leaf-stalk (petiole).

NODE. The part of a stem at which leaves and buds have their origin.

OVATE LEAVES. Shaped like a hen's egg, with the stem on the broader end.

PALMATE LEAVES. Leaves divided in a palm-like fashion.

PANICLE. A loose, spire-like group of flowers as in poinciana. An arrangement of racemes (which see).

PANS. Shallow clay pots generally used for growing bulbs, shallow-rooted plants, or germinating seed.

PISTIL. Central flower organ consisting of stem (style), apex (stigma), and ovary.

RACEME. A long cluster of flowers, each with its own stalk, and not close against the flower stems. It may be drooping, erect, loose, or compact depending upon the length of the stalks, as in Angelonia or Clianthus.

RHIZOME. A thickened underground stem that stores up food material and produces roots and stems of new plants at the joints.

SCAPE. Leafless flower stem rising from the soil, as in Lachenalia.

SPIKE. A long, spire-like flower cluster in which the individual flowers have no stalks and are borne close against the main flower stem as in Eucomis or Babiana.

SPUR. A projection from a flower. It may be tubular or saclike.

STAMEN. The pollen-bearing organ of the flower consisting of the anther and filament.

STYLE. The column in a flower extending above the ovary. It varies in length and is absent in some flowers.

TOP-DRESS. To remove exhausted soil from around the surface of a plant and replace it with new rich soil or well-rotted manure. Care should be taken not to harm roots when removing old soil.

TRUSS. A compact flower cluster at the end of a stem, as in Senecio.

UMBEL. Flower cluster with stems or rays arising from a common point like the frame work of an umbrella. Agapanthus and Nerine are good examples.

UNDULATED LEAVES. Wavy-margined or wavy-surfaced.

5

A to Z of Flowering Plants

ACALYPHA HISPIDA — REDHOT CATTAIL–CHENILLE PLANT

Red "Tails" of Bloom and Heart-shaped Leaves

An ornamental of unusual formation, with heart-shaped leaves and bright flowers that grow in long drooping tails, often to one foot. This novelty is sure to attract the attention of everyone who visits your greenhouse in the spring and summer. A. hispida is the popular flowering species with red or purplish tails extending from axils of leaves. Several other species are grown for colored foliage, and can be found in plant catalogs.

Moderate to warm greenhouse: 55° to 65°F.

Propagation: By cuttings taken from nearly mature growth at any time of the year. Plants started from February to April should reach small flowering size within a year. Several years are required to produce large specimens. An enclosed case with bottom heat at 70° to 75° gives cuttings a good start.

Potting: Transfer rooted cuttings to 3-inch pots. Peatmoss alone or peatmoss and loam suits them very well at this stage,

Passiflora alato-caerulea (Pfordtii), Passion Flower, page 130.

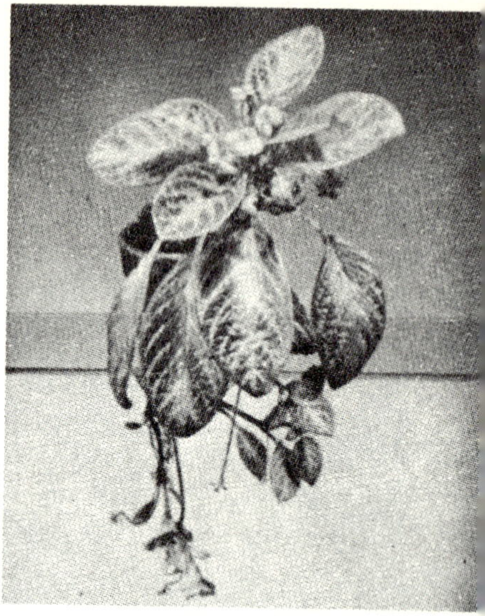

TOP LEFT: *Cyrtanthus Mackenii,* Ifafa Lily, page 74. TOP RIGHT: *Episcia,* page 79-80. BOTTOM LEFT: *Clerodendron Thomsoniae,* Glory Bower or Tree, page 65-66. BOTTOM RIGHT: *Jasminum,* page 109-110.

and when mature. Plants started in the spring should be ready for 5-inch pots by July. Pot firmly.

Culture: Shade through bright spring and summer weather, but in fall and winter, give all sunshine possible. Pinch the soft tips of the foliage to induce branching. Acalypha is essentially a warm greenhouse plant, and young plants do best at a night temperature of 65°. Mature plants can be carried over the winter at the moderate temperature of 55°. Water freely in spring and summer, moderately in autumn and winter.

Pests: Red spider and mealy bug.

Achania (See MALVAVISCUS.)

ACHIMENES

Velvet Bells for Hanging Baskets

Flowering plants closely related to gloxinias. They make a beautiful show in pots or hanging baskets from late spring to fall, and grow to 18 inches. Flowers are of velvety texture in tones of lavender, violet, and crimson. Varieties of drooping habit are excellent for baskets, but can also be grown in pans if staked and tied. A. longiflora major is the largest blooming variety with flowers 3 inches across, which open flat and are a vivid bright blue. A. patens is a dwarf compact grower with red flowers over an inch in diameter. A number of miscellaneous named hybrids are available.

Warm greenhouse: 60°F.

Propagation: By division of tubers before planting, from buds or offsets in the lower leaves, or from seed. Cuttings taken at a node also root easily in a mixture of peatmoss and sand during spring and summer. Grow them at a temperature of 60° to 65°. Offsets are treated and planted the same way as rhizomes, described below under *Culture.* Seed germinates at 75°, and is sown in January or February to produce flowering-sized plants by late fall. You can get many hybrids this way.

Potting: Transfer to 8-inch bulb pans or baskets as soon as growth is about 2 inches high, placing ten to twelve shoots in each container. Deep pots are not required, since Achimenes are shallow rooting.

Culture: Dormant tubers are started into growth in flats of peatmoss. Spread them out thinly in the peatmoss and set about 1 inch deep. Give 65° to 70° bottom heat for best rooting. Keep the moss moist but never wet or the tubers will rot. Transplant when growth is about 2 inches high. If the peatmoss that adheres to the roots can be left intact, the plants will get off to a better start.

You can have a succession of flowers by starting tubers in February, and making a second planting about five weeks later. Grow in a mixture of loose, fibrous, sandy loam that permits water to run off freely and provides good circulation of air—two-thirds well-rotted leafmold and peatmoss with one-third sand added is satisfactory, though some growers like to add up to one-third rotted manure to the mixture. Manure may be added in the form of top dressing after the plants have started. Some growers like to add peatmoss and a little sphagnum moss. They claim they can produce the largest tubers in this medium. I have used this mixture with excellent success.

Growth is rapid once it gets started and feeding every two weeks with a solution of ammonium sulphate—1 teaspoon to 1 gallon of water—or with a complete liquid fertilizer should be given when growth is 4 to 6 inches high. Grow at a temperature of 60° and continue feeding throughout the season. Shading from bright sunshine is essential. Do not permit the plants to suffer from dryness during flowering. Flowers will last longer if plants are kept cooler, at 50° to 55°, but never permit the temperature to go below 50°.

After flowering, let tubers remain for the winter in the same pots in which they grew. Lay the pots on their sides, and store under a bench if there is no danger of water from drainage. If space is at a premium, shake off the old soil, after the plants have dried, and store tubers in a box of dry sand and peatmoss. Paper bags are also good receptacles. The storage temperature should never be less than 45°.

Pests: Aphids, thrips, and red spider.

Aeschynanthus (See TRICHOSPORUM.)
African Hemp (See SPARMANNIA.)

AGAPANTHUS — BLUE AFRICAN LILY

Umbels of Blue Summer Lilies

A plant of the lily family. There are several dwarf varieties suitable for pot culture in the small greenhouse. Others are large and only worth while in large pots or small tubs. The blooms are light to dark blue or white, appearing in umbels or flat clusters on long stems above grassy or strap-shaped foliage. Flowers may come any time from late spring to early fall, but this plant is mostly summer blooming. A. africanus Mooreanus minor (Lily-of-the-Nile) is dwarf with umbels of blue flowers that give a lot of color. Intermedius is another low-growing form with the deepest of blue flowers. My Joy has bright blue flowers on 15-inch stems. Peter Pan is similar with clear blue flowers. Longispathus is a compact grower, very graceful and floriforous, with long pointed blue flowers. Many large flowering varieties are available.

Cool to moderate greenhouse: 45° to 55°F.

Propagation: By division of roots when repotting, or from seed that takes several years to reach flowering size.

Potting: Plant in 6-inch or larger pots, depending upon the size of the root stock and the plant wanted. Some dwarfs can be planted three to five rhizomes to a 6-inch pot. Tall varieties will take a 12-inch or larger pot or tub. Since this plant does best when pot bound and will not flower well when roots are disturbed, grow it on in the same pot for several years. Repot only when necessary, in the spring.

Culture: Plant in rich soil—two parts fibrous loam, one part leafmold or peatmoss, and one part decayed cow manure. Water well during spring and summer, but very little during fall and midwinter. This plant forces well, and can be brought into flower early by starting heavy watering and feeding with a complete fertilizer in February. Grow in full sunshine during the winter but shade from spring to fall.

Pests: This plant is rarely troubled with insects of any kind.

ALBUCA

White Fragrance for Early Spring

South African bulbous plant closely allied to ornithogalum. It bears large, white, heavily scented florets on the upper half of a 3-foot spike above flat, fleshy, basal foliage. A. crinifolia has pure white waxy blooms 2 inches across with a green midrib. A. Nelsonii is a handsome white species and much taller. Both bloom under glass in early spring.

Cool greenhouse: 45° to 50°F.

Propagation: By offsets from old bulbs taken when replanting, or from seed sown in spring.

Potting: Five bulbs set close together make a good 6-inch pot specimen. Ten bulbs may be planted in deep 8-inch pans, if a larger display is wanted. Replant in the fall.

Culture: In a fertile, well-drained, sandy soil, set bulbs with the upper third above the surface. Water well. Feed with liquid fertilizer after growth starts and during the active growing season. Keep in full sunlight all of the time. After flowering is over, permit foliage to ripen gradually; then store pots dry under a bench until the following season.

Pests: Thrips.

ALLAMANDA

Spring-to-Fall Show on a Climber

An evergreen climber, grown for large yellow or purplish, funnel-shaped flowers. This is one of the showiest climbers, and it flowers from late spring to fall. Unfortunately most varieties are too large for the small greenhouse. Dwarfs that are suitable include A. neriifolia (the oleander Allamanda), a semi-erect bush type that grows up to 3 feet, and A. violacea, a slender climber with flowers that are maroon in the center and bronze-red at the lower part. The yellow-flowering A. cathartica var. Williamsii is vigorous and more suited to a large greenhouse. It can be trained into bush form, however, and grown for several years in a small greenhouse.

Warm greenhouse: 60°F.

Propagation: By cuttings of half-ripened wood taken at any time of the year. They root best during March. Take cuttings with at least two or three joints and root in sand or soil at a temperature of 65°.

Potting: Pot young plants and cuttings as soon as they are rooted; then shift to 6's. Allamanda requires tighter potting than most plants or it will not succeed. Make full use of the potting stick when planting rooted cuttings or repotting mature plants. Continue to shift to larger pots as size of roots require. Repot mature plants just after new growth has started in spring, and before it is 6 inches long. Remove loose soil and use a pot 3 or 4 inches larger than the root ball because, when mature, the plant needs plenty of water and grows very fast. Allamanda is also successful in ground beds with plenty of drainage. The soil should be 12 to 15 inches deep. Place the bed up at the north end of the greenhouse or facing the workroom where it will not shade other plants.

Culture: Allamanda is one of the easiest greenhouse plants and does well in a fibrous loam of composted sand and manure, with sand added. A night temperature of 60° is essential; the plant will not do well at less than 50°. It is a heavy feeder, benefited by watering with a weak solution of ammonium sulphate or nitrate of soda—1 teaspoon to 1 gallon of water—or with a complete liquid fertilizer of any type that you prefer. Shading is not necessary except lightly during the warmest months.

When you grow the vigorous climbers, use a heavy, galvanized wire trellis. Each spring arrange most of the shoots over the lower section. Otherwise, rapid growth will cause all blooms to appear high up in the greenhouse. When growth has started, it is difficult to train plants, since stems are brittle and easily broken off.

After flowering, Allamanda must have a rest period. Hold back moisture gradually until leaves show signs of wilting. Continue drying off until about the end of October; then water enough to keep the season's young growth from shriveling. In mid-January, or before growth starts, cut the plant back to ripe wood.

Pests: Few insects attack Allamanda.

ALSTROMERIA

An Amaryllid of Rare Beauty

Tuberous-rooted plant with red, purple, or yellow blossoms in spring and summer. Though rarely grown under glass, this member of the amaryllis family is attractive and easy. A. Pelegrina alba is one of the best for pot culture with umbels of pure white flowers about 2 inches long. There are also many hybrids. Ask for greenhouse varieties when ordering.

Cool to warm greenhouse: 50° to 60°F.

Propagation: By division of roots or seed. Make divisions every year during January or February and plant in 4-inch or larger pots, as required. Sow seed thinly in pots or pans during August. Transplant to flats or pots as soon as seedlings are large enough to handle, for young plants incline to damp-off.

Potting: Transfer to 8- 10- or 12-inch pots provided with plenty of crock with a layer of sphagnum moss above; free drainage is essential. Repot during fall. Separate large roots from small ones. Grow the large roots for specimen plants, and start the smaller ones in pots of suitable size. Unless roots are divided in this way, they multiply so rapidly that good future growth is impossible.

Culture: A loose potting soil is needed. Use plenty of humus, such as composted sod or loam and manure. Water sparingly to bring into new growth slowly. Shade through the summer. Alstromeria will not tolerate direct sunshine. Plants may be set out in the garden where they will bloom through the summer. After foliage dies back in fall, keep plants on the dry side until March. Support stems by staking, when they are large enough, and mulch plants with peatmoss or rotted manure.

Pests: Red spider.

Amarcrinum (See CRINUM.)
Amazon Lily (See EUCHARIS.)

ANGELONIA SALICARIAEFOLIA

Bright Blue Flowers and Apple-Scented Foliage

A flowering shrub, 2 feet tall, blooming in late winter and spring, with great racemes of bright blue flowers, three-quarters of an inch across. The foliage is apple-scented.

Warm greenhouse: 60° to 65°F.

Propagation: By seed or softwood cuttings. Seed is rarely available, but the cuttings root readily at almost any time of year.

Potting: Plant rooted cuttings in 3-inch pots; transfer to 5's or 6's when large enough. After flowering, give fresh soil and a pot 2 inches larger.

Culture: Grow in fibrous loam lightened with decayed manure or peatmoss and sharp sand. Keep soil well moistened.

Pests: Thrips.

ANIGOZANTHUS FLAVIDA — AUSTRALIAN SWORD LILY–KANGAROO PAW

A Handsome Australian Amaryllid

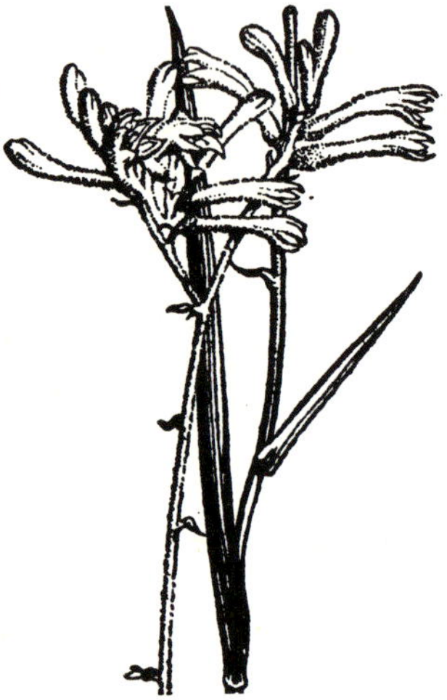

A fleshy rooted plant of the amaryllis family. Foliage resembles that of iris; numerous 1- to 3-inch tubular flowers open along one side of tall, well-branched stems during midwinter and early spring. A. flavida is yellow-green and blue-green. There are also orange-to-red hybrids and a variety, A. Manglesii, with red wool and green-red flowers.

Moderate to warm greenhouse: 55° to 60°F.

Propagation: By division of roots when repotting.

Potting: Grow in 4- to 7-inch pots, depending on size of rootstock. Repot in fresh soil every fall.

Culture: As with all members of this Australian family, a perfectly dry, dormant period after flowering is most important. Growth will start after a moderate watering late in fall, and from then on soil should be kept moderately moist. Plant in a mixture of loam, leafmold, and sand. Feed once or twice with a complete liquid fertilizer after growth starts, and keep in full sun all the time.

Pests: Aphids, red spider, scale, or mealy bug.

Anomatheca (See LAPEIROUSIA.)

FLOWERING ANTHURIUM

Exotic "Flowers" of Lasting Beauty

A plant with brilliant spathes or bracts, from which extend slender yellow or white spikes. The "flowers" in red, pink, rose, coral, orange, and white appear from March to August, and, under good conditions, each lasts for months. The large arrow- or heart-shaped leaves are also attractive. Shaffer hybrids are most popular. Those of the species, A. Scherzerianum, smaller and less exacting as to humidity, are easier than others like A. Andraeanum, which is also cataloged.

Warm greenhouse: 65°F.

Propagation: By suckers, or cuttings of rhizomes in January or February. Both root readily in a closed propagating bed at 75° to 80°. Seed germinates at 80°, but must have a constant dense humidity. It is best sown in February or March in a mixture of chopped sphagnum moss and sand.

Potting: Transplant young plants early since they are subject to damp-off. Select a 3- or 4-inch pot, depending on size of roots. Transfer to larger pots as necessary. Plants may be grown on in the same pots for three or four years.

Culture: Anthurium thrives in a mixture of peatmoss, broken-down osmundine fiber, sphagnum moss, and a little coarse sand. In such a medium, it will only have to be watered every two or three days. It does well under orchid-house conditions, since it must have dense humidity and shade, though it will not stand as much light as orchids. Flowers are produced from the axils of each vigorous leaf, and aerial roots push out at the base. Wrapping these roots with sphagnum moss keeps them alive and promotes better growth. Apply a complete liquid fertilizer once or twice in spring. Additional fertilizer is not needed. Special care should be taken to protect plants from drafts. Keep the roots very moist in spring and summer, but just moderately so the rest of the year.

Pests: Thrips and red spider.

ARDISIA CORAL ARDISIA

Coral Berries through the Year

A showy plant with small berries in brilliant drooping clusters. These appear intermittently following the insignificant white or rose flowers, and each abundant crop lasts a long time. A. crispa (crenata or crenulata) makes a neat compact shrub, and is the variety generally grown under glass. Six others are available.

Moderate to warm greenhouse: 55° to 65°F.

Propagation: By cuttings or seed in February or March. While plants are frequently raised from seed, propagation is quicker with cuttings of half-mature wood in a closed case at 70°. About a month is required. Seedlings do not usually make compact plants, and, unless selected with care, will not bear as many berries as plants from cuttings of good fruiting parents.

Potting: Transfer cuttings or seedlings to 3-inch pots. If potted in March, they should be ready for 5's by June, and 7's or 8's by August.

Culture: Plunge pots in sand or cinders. Do not attempt to grow plants on shelves, since they require a lot of moisture. Give full sunshine through the winter, but shade lightly in summer. Pinching is not necessary; plants branch of their own accord. A mixture of peatmoss, loam, and sand is satisfactory, but I like to grow Ardisia in straight peatmoss and sand. A temperature of 65° is needed for good growth in summer and fall; plants can be carried through the winter at 55°. Feed with ammonium sulphate—1 teaspoon to 1 gallon of water—or manure water, or a complete liquid fertilizer. Do not feed when flowers appear, and keep the temperature then at 55°, if possible. New growth at this stage of development will prevent setting of berries. After plants are two years old, a new generation should be started, for old plants get leggy and are not worth growing on.

Pests: Scale and mealy bug.

ARISTOLOCHIA ELEGANS CALICO FLOWER

A Vine with Fantastic Blooms

A slender greenhouse climber producing great, grotesque trumpets of bloom in late spring or summer. The plant is graceful and grows 8 to 10 feet high, but even when it is small, flowers appear on the new wood. Branches are pendulous with yellow-green blossoms, veined purple-white outside and purple-brown within. This species does not have the unpleasant odor of the others.

Moderate greenhouse: 55°F.

Propagation: By cuttings that root easily at any time of the year in peatmoss or sand. If taken in January, they will flower the following summer. Select well-matured wood and root in a closed case at 70°. Seed germinates readily and produces flowering plants the same year.

Potting: Transfer young cuttings to 3-inch pots. Pot firmly. Transfer to 6's when pots become crowded with roots. Plants started in January should be ready for 9-inch pots by October.

Culture: Aristolochia is a vigorous grower and does well in any porous soil. Maintain as high a humidity as possible and shade during the summer. Plants may be cut back to half-mature wood after flowering so they will not cast shade on other plants. Keep on the dry side during the winter, and repot or top-dress with fresh soil soon after growth starts in February. Never let plants suffer for want of water. Mature specimens in pots that are filled with roots will require watering once a day and a feeding every ten days with manure water or with a complete liquid fertilizer.

Pests: Scale, mealy bug, and red spider.

ARTHROPODIUM CIRRHATUM

White Stars for Winter

An evergreen herbaceous plant of the lily family. This attractive New Zealand native grows 3 feet high and in February or March produces starry white flowers about an inch across. They appear above grassy leaves on a well-branched panicle, about a foot long.

Cool greenhouse: 45° to 50°F.

Propagation: Freely by division after flowering or in October. Seed germinates readily in March.

Potting: Plant each division quite firmly in a 3-inch or larger pot depending on size and condition of roots. Transfer seedlings to 3's or 4's. Shift to larger pots when the first ones become filled with roots. This plant will never require more than a 6- to 8-inch pot. Repot mature plants in fresh soil after flowering.

Culture: Grow in fibrous loam lightened with leafmold, peatmoss, or well-rotted manure. Add coarse sand as required to provide free drainage. Give plenty of water when plants are growing and in bloom. Water less after flowering but never permit the soil to get dry. Maintain a high humidity and grow cool at all times. Shade lightly during summer.

Pests: Mealy bug.

Australian Sword Lily (See ANIGOZANTHUS.)

BABIANA — BABOON-ROOT

A Vivid South African Beauty

A cormous South African plant of the iris family, especially desirable for late winter or early spring bloom. Low-growing and of easy culture, this lance-leaved plant bears spiked clusters of six or so showy, pink, red, lilac, or purple flowers. Hybrids of B. stricta (illustrated) are excellent and most commonly seen; B. s. rubro-cyanea is also fine, growing up to 10 inches with dense spikes of vivid lilac flowers with red centers. Several other varieties are available.

Cool to moderate greenhouse: 50° to 55°F.

Culture: Treat the same as Ixia (which see).

Baboon-Root (See Babiana.)
Bellflower (See Campanula.)

BERGENIA CORDIFOLIA (SAXIFRAGA CORDIFOLIA)

A Creeper with Continuous Bloom

Large, shiny, elliptical leaves adorn this creeper and clusters of lavender-pink flowers appear almost continuously, but most freely during spring and summer. The plant grows rapidly, and can be handled either as a small or large specimen. Variety purpurea has panicles of reddish purple flowers.

Cool greenhouse: 50°F.

Propagation: By offshoots in spring and summer or divisions of rhizomatous roots in spring.

Potting: Pot according to size of division.

Culture: Bergenia does well in any well-drained soil. It should be watered moderately from spring to fall, kept on the dry side during winter, and shaded in summer.

Pests: Aphids and mealy bug.

Brodiaea uniflora (Triteleia uniflora), Spring Star Flower, page 50-51

TOP LEFT: *Chironia baccifera,* page 62. TOP RIGHT: *Vallota speciosa (purpurea),* Scarborough Lily, page 169-170. BOTTOM LEFT: *Crinum Powellii alba,* page 72-73. BOTTOM RIGHT: *Haemanthus multiflorus,* Blood Lily, page 90-91.

BESSERA ELEGANS CORAL-DROPS

Late Spring Brilliance

A distinguished member of the lily family from Mexico that is showy and ornamental. It is of easy culture and especially desirable for greenhouse forcing in the late spring. Drooping, brilliant, orange-red flowers marked creamy white appear in irregular clusters of five to ten blooms terminating the stem. Each bulb sends up several of these flower stems about 2 feet high, and, depending on size of bulb three or four can be planted to a 6-inch pot. This bulb is not to be confused with Milla biflora, a very different plant, that is sometimes sold under the same name.

Cool greenhouse: 50°F.

Culture: Treat the same as Ornithogalum (which see).

Bindweed (See CONVOLVULUS.)
Bird-of-Paradise (See STRELITZIA.)
Blood Lily (See HAEMANTHUS.)
Blue African Lily (See AGAPANTHUS.)
Blue Marguerite (See FELICIA.)
Blue Oxalis (See PAROCHETUS.)

BORONIA

Fragrance from a Dwarf Shrub

A hardwood dwarf shrub from Australia related to heather. Boronia makes a most desirable flowering plant for pot culture. Terminal branches are covered with clusters of fragrant red or purple blooms from the end of March well into June. The graceful foliage is attractive even when the plant is not in flower. B. heterophylla is the most prolific bloomer and easiest to grow. It bears bright, fragrant, rose-colored blooms and is more attractive than B. megastigma, the other popular variety, which has maroon-purple flowers with yellow centers.

Cool greenhouse: 45° to 50°F.

Propagation: By cuttings and seeds in spring. Cuttings 3 to 4 inches long are taken in fall and rooted in sand, or in a mixture of sand and peatmoss at a temperature of 55°. Seed is difficult to germinate (I tried and failed), but it is said to produce flowering-sized plants in a year.

Potting: Transfer small plants to 2- or 3-inch pots. Be sure to set firmly. Under no circumstances allow plants to become pot-bound, but shift to 4's or 5's as soon as required. By summer, cuttings started in fall will be ready to transfer to 6's or 7's. Plants flower when quite young, but should be repotted the following summer in 8-inch pots.

Culture: A mixture of one third fibrous loam with two parts coarse peatmoss and sand has been recommended, but I prefer a mixture of peatmoss and sand that provides good drainage. This is important, for Boronia will not stand soggy conditions. Syringing is beneficial in bright weather when the house can be ventilated, but it must be done with care since foliage is susceptible to mildew. Plants may be grown outdoors in summer, if they are protected from burning sunshine and driving rains. Place pots in a warm place in the greenhouse in the fall. Plants make the best growth at 55° at this season. Frequent pinching is essential, especially in the early stages, to develop well-formed plants. Cut back after flowering to keep compact.

Pests: Brown scale and aphids.

BOUGAINVILLEA

Tropical Brilliance in Spring

A flowering climber or shrub for the small, medium-sized, or large greenhouse. Plants can be grown in large pots or tubs. Flowers are inconspicuous but they are surrounded by large bracts that make a brilliant display in April, May, and sometimes June. Sanderiana, the Paper Flower, a variety of B. glabra, is an excellent purple species; Crimson Lake, a variety of B. spectabilis, is bright crimson. Both are well suited to pot culture. Other hybrids are available.

Warm greenhouse: 60°F.

Propagation: By cuttings, 5 to 6 inches long, that root readily in spring either in small pots of peatmoss and sand or in a propagating bed. Such cuttings should make 6-inch pot plants by September and be ready to force into flower the following April.

Potting: Transfer into small pots as soon as rooted, and then directly into 5's or 6's. Repot mature plants just after new growth starts in fall.

Culture: A coarse soil mixture of peatmoss, loam, and leaf-mold, with sand added, suits Bougainvillea very well. Feed with liquid fertilizer to get as much growth as possible before October; then keep on the dry side, since buds form on ripened wood in the short days between September twentieth and October first. After flowering is over, cut back growth made during the season so that only 2 to 3 inches remains. Plants kept on the dry side will stay dormant for a long time, yet may be brought into growth quickly if soaked in water and grown at 60°. They may be plunged out in the garden in summer.

Pests: Mealy bug, scale, and red spider.

BRODIAEA SPRING STAR FLOWER

Fragrant Spring Trumpets

A semi-hardy, flowering cormous plant. In early spring, loose clusters of soft, funnel-shaped blooms appear. Stems are wiry, about a foot long, with a few graceful leaves near the base. The blooms are small, so quite a number of plants are needed for a nice display. The Spring Star Flower, B. uniflora (triteleia and leucocoryne), is white, tinted blue. Ixioides (Pretty Face) is salmon-yellow tinged with dark purple. A number of other colorful varieties are available.

Moderate greenhouse: 55°F.

Propagation: By offsets or seed. Offsets should be left undisturbed on the parent plant until they reach flowering size and may be separated in the fall. Plants from seed take several years to flower.

Potting: Pot corms in September about 2 inches apart in a 6- or 7-inch pan. Water sparingly until growth starts.

Culture: Grow in poor, well-drained, sandy soil. These bulbs do best in soil that is not rich or heavy with organic matter and nutrients. Give plenty of sunshine and dry off gradually after flowering. Store corms throughout the summer in the same manner as Ixias, which see.

Pests: Aphids and thrips.

BROMELIADS

Flowers in the Pineapple Family

A group of plants of the pineapple family, including Aechmea, Billbergia, Cryptanthus, Tillandsia, Vriesia, Neoregelia, and many more genera. The brilliant bracts and blooms appear in striking combinations of colors. So popular have these bromeliads become that many plantsmen devote considerable catalog space to them; there is even a Bromeliad society. Some of the rare varieties are costly, but less expensive ones are found in the genera Billbergia, Cryptanthus, Aechmea, and Neoregelia. A beginner might start with these.

Warm greenhouse: 60° to 65°F.

Billbergia is the favorite of this group. Its pastel flowers offer delicate contrast to the vivid-hued bracts. The stiff leaves, usually in rosettes, may be gray-banded, striped, or mottled. Flower spikes come from the center and varieties differ considerably in form: some produce dense flower heads; most are more or less loose and elegantly drooped. Blooming periods vary, but fall to spring is usual.

There are too many good species and hybrids for me to give a long list of recommendations, so I mention only a few of the most desirable. You will find a wider assortment in the catalogs. Billbergia nutans, the Queen's Tears, is the most common. It has narrow, silvery green foliage and rose bracts. Four to eight flowers combine in drooping clusters of green, edged with purple. Pyramidalis is vase-shaped and has the exotic combination of olive-green leaves, dense spikes with red bracts, and rose flowers tipped purple. Zebrina is tall, tubular, and stiff. Its striking foliage is gray with silver-white bands on the outside.

Aechmea miniata discolor, the Living Vase, has glossy leaves, green above, maroon below, and a red berried flower head with light blue petals. Aechmea racinae, Christmas Jewels, has a pendant inflorescence of bright red, yellow, and black. Aechmea Orlandiana is a handsome species with black mottlings on light green leaves. It blooms in midwinter with an orange and white cluster of flowers.

The Cryptanthus genus is composed of low-sprawling starfish rosettes. They are of different colors with bands or striped. Small white flower clusters in the middle of the plant barely rise above central leaves. Zonatus, bivittatus, and beuckerii are attractive species; their hybrids are also interesting.

The Tillandsia group is the largest genus in the bromeliad family, but few are generally known. Lindenii, though still rare, is one of the most beautiful of all cultivated bromeliads. Large blue iris-like flowers emerge from the side of a flat pink and green spike. Spanish Moss, Tillandsia usneoides, is a member of this tribe. Ionantha is a spectacular miniature when it flowers in spring. Fasciculata is unusual with narrow blue-gray leaves, brilliant red bracts, and blue flowers.

Neoregelias are both rugged and decorative. They are very good greenhouse or house plants and their colorful leaves make them a year-round attraction. Carolinae has narrow, light green leaves and a brilliant cerise cup with a head of blue flowers, low in the center. Farinosa, Crimson Cup, has wider leaves of bronze-green and makes a gorgeous display in the spring. Spectabilis is the well-known "fingernail" plant with red-tipped leaves. Marmorata has olive-green leaves marbled with maroon and brown. It also has red foliage tips.

Vriesias are closely related to Tillandsias. Many of them flower longer than any other bromeliad. The carinata hybrid, Marie, is a symphony in red, green, and yellow from Thanksgiving through Easter. Carinata, one of the parents of Marie, is smaller, blooms a bit earlier, and is equally attractive. For dramatic foliage there are splendens and hieroglyphica with dark, purple-banded leaves. Most of the other Vriesias have plain green leaves, but interesting flat spikes of inflorescence.

Nidularium, Quesnelia, Hohenbergia, and Guzmania are less known genera but all have spectacular members to grow under glass.

Most of the bromeliads are attractive in form all through the year and have an added dividend of flowering from three weeks to six months. Bromeliads make a colorful, exciting addition to any collection of tropical plants.

Propagation: By shoots or suckers that grow from the base of the plant after it has flowered. These root any time of year, but take hold most easily in April, when they are usually about a fourth as large as the parent plant. Cut the shoot off close to the base. Shoots may even have roots attached. Plant in loose, sandy, fibrous loam, using pots just large enough to take them. Place them in the warmest spot in the greenhouse, since a temperature of 65° to 70° is desirable. Do not try to root bromeliads in a propagating case having a high humidity, for they rot if kept too wet.

Potting: Transfer plants to pots 2 to 3 inches larger, after roots are well formed. A shift to containers 2 inches larger will be necessary in the summer. Pots, clay pans, or wire baskets are used. Further repotting should not be necessary until plants make vigorous growth, unless you wish to grow them in larger groups. Old parent plants may throw out additional suckers but once flowered, the size of plants will not increase. The old plant may live for another year if all shoots are not detached.

Culture: A potting medium that drains freely is essential. Some collectors grow bromeliads in osmundine, but a mixture of equal parts of sand, leafmold, and peatmoss is more popular and economical. While not much moisture is needed at the roots during the winter, varieties having funnel-like cups should have these filled with water all year. The plant draws on this as it needs to. During spring and summer, when in growth, plenty of water is also needed at the roots. Too much direct sunshine may destroy the foliage, but too much shade will prevent the rich coloration of foliage. Bromeliads need plenty of light and ventilation, and, when making growth, are benefited by feeding with a complete liquid fertilizer every ten days to two weeks. They can stand considerable abuse and during cool weather will go for long periods without water.

This makes them desirable houseplants, but they do much better in a greenhouse.

Pests: Bromeliads are rarely troubled by insects.

BRUNFELSIA (FRANCISCEA) LADY-OF-THE-NIGHT

For Intense Fragrance

A fall-to-spring flowering shrub native to the West Indies. The long slender tubes grow singly or in loose clusters; both formations have exceptional beauty. Fragrance is particularly intense at night. Under glass, Brunfelsia reaches 3 to 4 feet. The luxuriant foliage shows the blooms off to fine advantage. B. calycina variety macrantha is the most popular greenhouse species and is fairly easy to grow. Its flowers are a rich, deep purple with a prominent lavender ring and white eye. Many other varieties are available.

Warm greenhouse: 60°F.

Propagation: By cuttings of ripened wood taken during the spring or fall. Root in a mixture of peat and sand or vermiculite.

Potting: Transfer singly to small pots. Then shift to 6's until flowering size is reached. Repot in 8's after flowering. Top dress with fresh soil each spring thereafter.

Culture: Grow in a rich, loose compost and feed with liquid fertilizer or manure every two weeks during the growing season. This feeding is essential to mature plants that are somewhat pot-bound. Flowers last longer if the house is kept cool, but growth is faster at a temperature of 55°. Prune lightly before new growth starts. Syringe during bright summer weather until buds form.

Pests: Mealy bug and scale.

BRUNSVIGIA

Pink, Rose, or White Lilies in Clusters

A bulb of the amaryllis family with umbels of numerous large flowers. It can be brought into bloom in winter and spring. Leaves are strap-shaped, about 2 feet high, and like the amaryllis, usually do not appear until after the plant has bloomed. The fragrant pink flowers of B. rosea major come early and are unusually large, as are those of the dark pink B. rosea parkeri. B. rosea Hathor is a pure white lily of rare beauty.

Warm greenhouse: 60° to 65°F.

Propagation: By offsets or seed. Plant offsets in rich fibrous loam; it may take them two years to reach flowering size. Sow seeds in pans of fine vermiculite at 60°. Set young plants singly in 3-inch pots. Shift to larger sizes as required, keeping the young bulbs well covered with soil.

Potting: Grow in bulb pans or pots about 2 inches larger than the bulbs, which are 3 to 6 inches in diameter. After drying off bulbs, repot at the beginning of each season.

Culture: Bulbs are usually available in November and December, and should be planted immediately after they are received. Grow in a rich, loose, fibrous soil with 2-10-10 commercial fertilizer added, at the rate of one 4-inch potful to 2 bushels of soil. These bulbs like plenty of potash. The soil should be kept moderately moist until growth starts. Feed with ammonium sulphate—1 teaspoon to 1 gallon of water—every three weeks up to a short time after flowering. Keep the foliage growing as long as possible until early summer, when bulbs should be dried off. However, do not remove from the old pots until the following fall. In replanting, remove only the dead roots. Preserve the live fleshy ones which will take hold and continue to grow.

Pests: Aphids, green fly, scale, and mealy bug.

Bryophyllum (See KALANCHOE.)
Butterfly Pea (See CLITORIA.)
Caesalpinia (See POINCIANA.)
Calico Flower (See ARISTOLOCHIA.)
California Geranium (See SENECIO.)

CAMPANULA ISOPHYLLA — BELLFLOWER

Dainty Flowers for Baskets

A perennial, desirable for its long blooming season, from spring until fall. It is most attractive in hanging baskets. C. isophylla (erroneously called Star-of-Bethlehem) has numerous pale blue, bell-shaped flowers. Variety alba is white; Mayi bears larger white blooms.

Moderate to warm greenhouse: 55° to 60°F.

Propagation: By division or basal cuttings in February, or by seed sown in March at a temperature of 60°. Shade young plants from hot sun. Transfer seedlings to flats about 1½ inches apart as soon as they are large enough to handle. Special care in watering is essential, for these Bellflowers are subject to damp-off and will not stand too much water on the foliage.

Potting: Divisions and rooted cuttings are grown in 3-inch or larger pots depending upon size. Mature plants are grown in 5-inch and larger pots, or hanging baskets lined with sphagnum moss.

Culture: Plants require little attention other than shading from the hot sun during the spring and summer, and care in watering during the short days of fall and winter. A light, rich soil that has been composted with manure suits them very well. In spring, feed once or twice with manure water or a solution of ammonium sulphate or nitrate of soda—1 teaspoon to a gallon of water. With moderate care, the plants grow on year after year.

Pests: Aphids and green fly.

Cape Cowslip (See LACHENALIA.)
Cape Honeysuckle (See TECOMARIA.)
Cape Marigold (See DIMORPHOTHECA.)
Cape Primrose (See STREPTOCARPUS.)

CASSIA CORYMBOSA — SENNA

Yellow "Sweet Peas" for Beginners

An evergreen shrub of easy culture, excellent for beginners. Yellow, pea-shaped terminal clusters appear in spring, summer, or autumn. In maturity, foliage grows 4 to 10 feet and is itself most attractive. This plant will flower when quite small.

Warm greenhouse: 60°F.

Propagation: By cuttings from half-mature wood in March. These will bloom the following fall. Root in peatmoss and sand at 80°.

Potting: Transfer rooted cuttings to 4-inch pots. When ready, pot firmly in 6's or 8's. Plants will not require shifting for two or three years, unless very large specimens are wanted. Do not disturb the roots when repotting.

Culture: Cassia is not particular as to soil and can be grown in ordinary garden loam. Pinch off straggling growth. Feed with manure water or complete fertilizer every ten days until well-established; then once or twice during the spring. Shade during hot summer weather, but grow in full sunshine the rest of the year. Prune back to half-mature wood in late fall. Then keep on the dry side and grow cool, 45° to 50°, until ready to force at 60° in March.

Pests: Red spider, thrips, and green fly.

CATESBAEA SPINOSA — LILY THORN

A Double-Feature Shrub

An evergreen shrub from the West Indies. White or cream trumpets, as long as 6 inches, hang underneath the branches from January to spring, and even into summer. They are followed by yellow berries. This shrub is slow-growing and flowers when only 8 to 10 inches high. Eventually it will require a small tub because it grows to 4 or 5 feet.

Warm greenhouse: 65°F.

Culture: Treat the same as Clerodendron speciosissimum (which see), but keep slightly on the dry side.

CENTROPOGON

Handsome Crimson Basket Plant

A shrubby creeper of the lobelia family. It grows quickly and is excellent for hanging baskets or edging benches. There is a prolific crop of bright crimson flowers during midwinter. These appear from bracts at the end of each stem. They are small, tubular, and double-lipped in a beautiful raceme covering about one-half the ends of the stems. A very striking effect is possible when the stems are spread out and supported part way with bamboo stakes. Then the ends arch down and flowers stand erect above the leaves so the color stands out most effectively. Since this plant is one of the most attractive of the winter bloomers, it is surprising that it is not more generally grown.

Warm greenhouse: 60° to 65°F.

Propagation: By cuttings in March that root at a temperature of 70° to 75°.

Potting: Plant 4 to 6 plants to a 6- or 8-inch basket or pan. For bench edging, plant 4 to 5 inches apart.

Culture: Use a light porous soil, such as loam and peatmoss with a little sand added. Water freely when the plant is making growth, and shade from June to September. Feed with liquid fertilizer every two weeks during the growing period. Keep only moderately moist during the short days of January and February, but never so dry that leaves wilt.

Pests: Aphids.

CESTRUM

For Early Spring Color and Fragrance

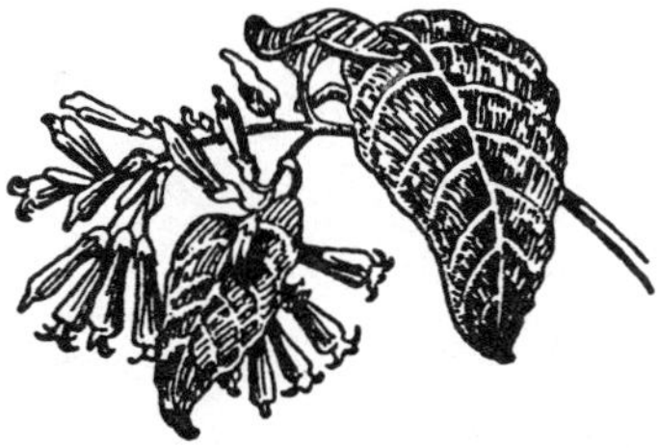

A distinctive evergreen shrub or semi-climber with clusters of bright, showy flowers that look like jasmine. They appear over a long period through late spring and summer, and start when plants are quite small. C. aurantiacum has orange-red flowers, C. purpureum or elegans (illustrated), and C. fasciculatum, purple-red ones. C. duirnum, nocturnum, and Parqui are grown for their enchanting fragrance at night.

Warm greenhouse: 60° to 65°F.

Culture: Treat the same as Bougainvillea (which see).

Pests: Mealy bug.

Chenille Plant (See ACALYPHA.)
Chilean Crocus (See TECOPHILAEA.)
China Rose (See HIBISCUS.)
Chinese Hat Plant (See HOLMSKIOLDIA.)

CHIRONIA BACCIFERA

Dainty and Pink from Spring to Summer

A perennial from South Africa with lovely pink spring-to-summer flowers that look like gentians. They are followed by scarlet berries. C. baccifera, the only variety I find available, makes a well-branched plant that grows to 2 feet high.

Cool greenhouse: 50°F.

Propagation: By seed or cuttings. The best plants are grown from cuttings taken in February. They root easily in sandy soil at a temperature of 50° and start to flower by late spring. Seed takes a year to produce flowering-sized plants.

Potting: Transfer small plants to 3-inch pots and try to get them up to a 5-inch size before winter. Be careful not to overpot or the soil may become wet and soggy.

Culture: Grow in loose sandy soil of one part fibrous loam with three parts peatmoss and plenty of coarse sand for good drainage. Shading during the spring and summer is essential; otherwise very little attention is required.

Pests: Aphids.

CHOISYA TERNATA — MEXICAN ORANGE-FLOWER

For Orange-Blossom Fragrance

An evergreen shrub that flowers from spring to summer. C. ternata, the only species, grows 3 to 6 feet tall, and on the terminal shoots it bears white, sweet-scented flowers that resemble orange blossoms. They stand out in elegant contrast to the shiny leathery leaves.

Sinningia Buell Hybrid, Gloxinia, page 148-149.

Fuchsia Hybrid, Ladies-Ear-Drops, page 85-86.

Cool to moderate greenhouse: 45° to 55°F.

Propagation: By cuttings of almost mature shoots any time from spring to fall. Cuttings 3 to 4 inches long root readily in peat-moss and sand or vermiculite at 55° to 65°. Bottom heat and a closed case or bell jar hasten rooting, or cuttings can be set directly in small pots plunged in peatmoss or sand. Shade until well-rooted, then pot in a mixture of loam, peatmoss or leaf-mold, and a small quantity of sand.

Potting: Transfer to 6-inch pots when plants are large enough, then on to 10- or 12-inch pots, using the soil mixture described above. Repot old plants in the fall, or when new growth starts in February, or top-dress with new soil and well-rotted manure.

Culture: Rest plants in the fall by withholding water for about 2 months. Then, as new shoots appear, water well. Never let plants lack water when making growth. Syringe the foliage on bright days, except when plants are in flower. From late spring to fall feed both young and well-established plants with manure water or ammonium sulphate—1 teaspoon to 1 gallon of water. Plants may be set outdoors during the summer with pots plunged to hold moisture. To keep plants in good condition, prune straggly growth after the flowers have past. Move plants into the greenhouse again during September. In a 45°-house, plants will blossom during late spring or summer. At 55°, they bloom in March. Some gardeners claim Choisya can be brought into flower every two or three months by withholding water to harden growth at a temperature of 45°, then watering well and raising the temperature to 55°. I have never been successful in getting it to flower during the winter.

Pests: Red spider.

CHORIZEMA

Clusters of Brilliant "Sweet Peas"

A hardwood evergreen flowering shrub. This is one of the most striking you can grow either as a pot plant, which will reach to 4 feet high, or as a semi-climber up to 10 feet. Blossoms look like sweet peas. The clusters are set off by the holly-like foliage. Chorizema flowers profusely in spring and early summer, and, with proper handling, can be kept in partial bloom during the winter. C. cordatum, a tall slender shrub, bears long clusters of scarlet flowers. C. varium, with light orange flowers, is more compact and especially prolific.

Propagation: By cuttings or seed. Cuttings of half-ripened wood root quickly in a mixture of two parts sand and one part peatmoss at a temperature of 60°. Take them during the spring to get good 6-inch plants by fall. These will flower the following spring. Transplant to 3-inch pots when rooted. Straight peatmoss is best during this stage of growth. Seed sown in February or March germinates readily at a temperature of 65° to 70°.

Potting: Move to 6-inch pots before the small pots become crowded with roots. Use a fibrous sod loam with one-third peatmoss and just a little sand. Plants will be ready for 10's or 12's by spring.

Culture: Pinch young plants two or three times to induce branching, and shade from bright sunshine. Feed with liquid manure or a complete liquid fertilizer every two weeks. During bright, hot weather, shading and daily syringing will keep plants in good condition. Straggly growth will need pinching to develop a compact form. Plants grown as tall semi-climbers are pinched to three or four stems and trained on wires. Feed mature plants with liquid manure or ammonium sulphate—1 teaspoon to 1 gallon of water—every other week until flower buds set in September and October. At this time growth will slow up. Remove shading and discontinue syringing in October. Repotting, when necessary, is best done during January or February, but plants will grow in the same pot for several years, if well fed.

Pests: Red spider if grown under dry conditions, brown scale.

CLERODENDRON — GLORY-BOWER, GLORY-TREE

A Grand Show with Little Trouble

A vigorous shrub which grows up to 4 feet, or a twiner up to 10 feet. It will flourish with less attention than most plants you try. The large showy panicles appear over a long period in early spring or summer. Colors range from white to violet, scarlet, or red. Old plants may get too large for a small greenhouse, but young plants can be brought into flower in any size pot from a 6- to an 8-inch. C. Thomsoniae (Balfouri) is one of the most beautiful of greenhouse climbers with rich crimson flowers handsomely set off by white calyxes. This one grows to 10 feet but flowers when the plant is only 18 inches high. C. fragrans is bushy, from 2 to 6 feet, with fragrant white flowers. It can be forced at cooler temperatures than most of the others. C. speciosissimum (fallax) has graceful, dull-red blooms and grows 2 to 4 feet high. C. Bungei, with rose-red upright clusters, makes a shrub from 3 to 6 feet high.

Warm greenhouse: 65°F.

Propagation: By cuttings of half-ripened wood or seed in January or February. Cuttings about 6 inches long are rooted in sand, a mixture of sand and peatmoss, or vermiculite, and grown at 70°. Shrubby varieties root faster than the twiners, and require less attention. Twiners are more easily managed in a closed case. Maintain a high humidity and syringe daily to keep the foliage fresh. Seed germinates readily at 70° to 75°. Plants from either seed or cuttings will reach flowering size the following spring.

Potting: Transfer rooted cuttings to 3-inch pots. Pot firmly. Growth is rapid and the plants will soon be ready for 5's or 6's. The following spring, transfer to 10's, and from then on to the size pot desired, up to a 20-inch tub. Repot after a little new growth has started or top-dress with fresh soil.

Culture: Clerodendron will thrive best in a coarse, composted, sod loam with one fifth sharp sand added. Feed the plants every ten days during the growing period with manure water, ammonium sulphate—1 teaspoon to 1 gallon of water—or a complete liquid fertilizer. The blossoms come on new growth, so it is not necessary to harden plants off. During spring and summer, shade the plants and syringe the foliage twice a day. Never let them lack water until after flowering in October. Rest the plants by keeping them on the dry side from October to January; then give just enough water to prevent the leaves from wilting. During this period, a temperature of 55° to 60° is desirable. Soak the plants well in January and February, and force at a temperature of 65° for blooms in March or April. Prune plants after flowering. The bushy shrub type can be cut back considerably, so they take little space in the greenhouse during the dormant period. If the plants are dried off for six weeks to two months, they can be brought into flower again in the fall.

Pests: Mealy bug and aphids.

CLIANTHUS DAMPIERI — GLORY PEA, DESERT PEA

Most Beautiful of Basket Plants

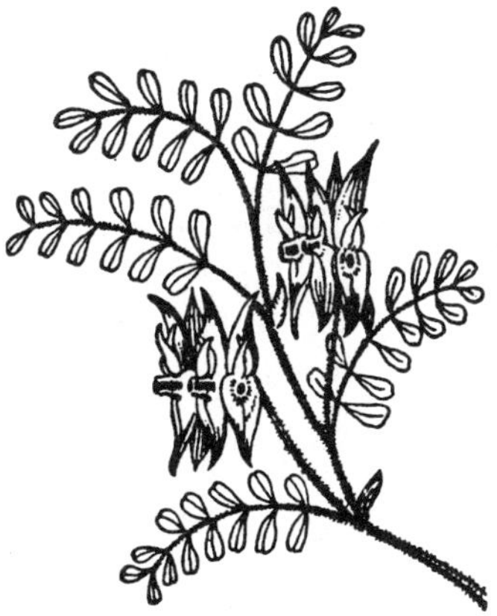

A creeper of extraordinary beauty. Although it is difficult, it is worth your effort. The lovely silvery foliage hangs 2 to 4 feet. The large flowers are bright red with a velvety, purplish black spot at the base. They appear in drooping racemes from the axils of each vigorous leaf. It is the most attractive basket plant I know, even though it blooms for only a short time in spring.

Cool greenhouse: 45° to 50°F.

Propagation: By cuttings or seed in February or March. Seed germinates at 75°. Avoid frequent moving by sowing seed singly in a 5-inch pot. Cuttings root at 75° to 80°, but most plants you buy will be grafted on Colutea arborescens seedlings.

Potting: This plant is fastidious when young and needs plenty of root space, so grow it in an 8- or 10-inch basket or pot. Avoid disturbing the soil, since root injury may kill the plant.

Culture: Exceptionally good drainage is essential. Use a rich, sandy loam and leafmold. Give abundant sunshine and moderate watering from September to early spring, but light shade, daily syringing, and liberal watering during late spring and summer. Cut back after flowering.

Pests: Red spider and scale.

CLITORIA TERNATEA BUTTERFLY PEA

Constant Blue from a Climber

A shrubby climber with brilliant, sky-blue flowers which look like sweet peas and are about 1-inch long. It blooms freely but intermittently through the year. Any variety you find available should be satisfactory, but one plant will be adequate for your greenhouse. It is a rapid grower but not difficult to keep under control.

Warm greenhouse: 65°F.

Culture: It is not particular as to soil. Six-inch flowering plants may be produced from seed within a year. Treat the same as Passiflora (which see).

CLIVIA

Clusters of Orange and Yellow Trumpets

A flowering plant of the amaryllis family with evergreen foliage. It is often seen in collections at flower shows where fine specimens never fail to attract attention. Blooms make a striking show in winter and spring, the bright clusters radiating from a stiff upright stem about 2 feet high. C. miniata has the typical showy, soft orange-yellow blooms, but hybrids, such as cyrtanthiflora with pleasing variations of color, are most commonly grown.

Warm greenhouse: 60°F.

Propagation: By seed or offsets. Seed germinates readily and many hybrids are produced this way. However, since five or seven years are needed to produce plants from seed, only hybridizers will have the patience to raise them. Division of the fleshy roots is done when plants are repotted, but it must be remembered that they do best when roots are undisturbed for a year or more.

Potting: Pot small bulbs in 6-inch or larger pots, depending upon the root development. Firm potting is essential. Older plants will require 8's, 10's or 12's. A top-dressing with fresh soil in the spring is preferable to repotting, which may disturb the roots.

Culture: Clivia requires a rich, fibrous loam that drains freely, and a temperature of 60° to make growth in spring. The optimum is 45° to 50° for resting during fall and winter. While little water is required in winter, the plant should not become so dry that leaves show signs of wilting. Give plenty of water just as soon as growth starts, and feed every week with liquid manure or ammonium sulphate—1 teaspoon to 1 gallon of water. Shade is always essential with the possible exception of December to February. Bright sun will burn off the foliage.

Pests: Mealy bug.

COLUMNEA GLORIOSA

Scarlet Trailer for Summer

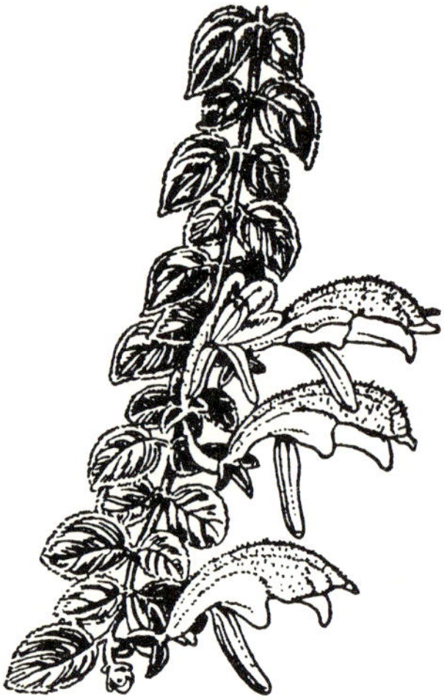

An evergreen plant from Costa Rica of the same Gesneria family as gloxinias, achimenes, and African violets. Long and trailing, it is well suited to hanging baskets, though with a light wire trellis it may also be grown upright. The large, velvety leaves are rather fleshy and covered with purple hairs. The large scarlet-and-yellow flowers rise from the axils of the vigorous leaves, and are most numerous near the ends of the stems. This Columnea has a long summer season of bloom.

Warm greenhouse: 60° to 70°F.

Culture: Treat the same as Trichosporum (which see).

Confederate Jasmine (See TRACHELOSPERMUM.)

CONVOLVULUS BINDWEED

Perennial Morning Glories for Your Greenhouse

An excellent twiner for those who want something different for hanging baskets or pots. In spring or summer, C. Cneorum bears white flowers tinged with pink. C. mauritanicus is not a vine; it grows to about 7 inches and is everblooming with handsome, deep violet-purple flowers with a lighter throat.

Moderate greenhouse: 55°F.

Propagation: In February from seed that blooms by summer, or cuttings that produce spring-flowering plants. Plant four or five seeds in a 5-inch pot, and save one or two of the strongest seedlings.

Potting: Grow on in the same pots in which seeds were started, or when seedlings are 3 to 4 inches long, transfer to hanging baskets lined with sphagnum moss.

Culture: Convolvulus does best in a soil that has considerable fiber, such as composted sod, or soil and manure. Give plenty of sunshine throughout the winter, but shade lightly during spring and summer. Feed young plants once or twice with a good liquid fertilizer or with manure water. Additional feeding is not necessary since they grow vigorously.

Pests: Aphids and green fly.

Coral Ardisia (See ARDISIA.)
Coral-Drops (See BESSERA.)
Coral Plant (See RUSSELIA.)

CORYTHOLOMA CARDINALIS

Bright Sprays of Velvet Blooms

A tuberous-rooted, May-blooming plant allied to the gloxinia. It has leafy stems, soft, hairy leaves, and red velvet flowers about 3 inches long. They grow in terminal clusters or sprays.

Warm greenhouse: 65°F.

Culture: Treat the same as gloxinia. (See SINNINGIA.)

CRASSULA LACTEA

Dependable for Winter

Here is one variety of crassula you can count on to flower for a long time in midwinter. It makes a handsome well-branched plant about 2 feet tall with spotted leaves connected at the base. Blooms are small, but numerous in white, flat-topped clusters.

Cool to moderate greenhouse: 50° to 55°F.

Culture: Treat the same as Kalanchoe (which see).

CRINUM AND AMARCRINUM

Form, Color, and Fragrance

A tropical bulbous amaryllid with fragrant umbels—six to twelve on long stems. They vary in form from erect, lily-like trumpets to drooping, starry sprays. All are characterized by a long tube. While most of the crinums become extremely large plants, they can be handled in pots. Under glass, blooms are possible from April to summer, in soft pink to purple, wine to red, and white streaked with pink or red.

Amarcrinum is a handsome hybrid between Brunsvigia and C. Moorei with amaryllis-like flowers in large clusters. The winter and early spring flowers are exquisitely perfumed. C. Powelli alba and C. giganteum are excellent pure whites. C. Ellen Bousanquet, one of the most beautiful of all, is a deep wine-red. C. scabrum is white and crimson, and Amarcrinum Howardii, a soft pink. Many other hybrids are available.

Moderate to warm greenhouse: 55° to 65°F.

Propagation: By offsets taken when repotting. Seeds sown in the spring take three or four years to produce blooming-sized plants.

Potting: Plant with half the bulb above the surface of the soil. Repot every three to four years in March. Plant offsets in 3- or 4-inch pots and give plenty of heat and moisture. The varieties mentioned can be handled for a few years in 7- or 8-inch pots, and those of small-blooming size can be grown in 6's, with the bulb resting almost on the surface of the soil. Later they may require up to 10- or 12-inch pots. Crinums need repotting only every three or four years.

Culture: Grow in a sandy soil with peatmoss, leafmold, or sphagnum moss. Plants do best in acid soil and are inclined to turn yellow from chlorosis in soils that are alkaline. Good drainage is essential, if plants are to go for several years without repotting. Store dry under benches from fall to midwinter, watering moderately during January or February to encourage growth. Water freely after growth starts, and feed once every two weeks with weak liquid fertilizer. Shade lightly from the hot sun of June to September, and syringe daily. If plants incline to too much top growth, give them more light. It will reduce foliage area and check climbing. C. Moorei is an exception. Direct summer sun will burn off its foliage just as it does that of Clivias.

Amarcrinums can be dried off like amaryllis, and Crinums can be handled the same way, if space is at a premium. Since both are evergreen, they may be grown in the greenhouse through the year, and their foliage will prove decorative.

Pests: Red spider, scale, mealy bug, and thrips.

Cypella (See IRIS FAMILY.)

CYRTANTHUS IFAFA LILY

White, Yellow, or Orange Flowers from a Bulb

A South African bulb of the amaryllis family. This makes an excellent pot plant with slender, waxy flowers in pendulous or erect clusters from late winter to early spring. Popular varieties include: C. lutescens with glossy, soft, yellow flowers; C. Mackenii, an ivory-white; and C. Howardii, a reddish-orange.

Cool to warm greenhouse: 50° to 60°F.

Propagation: By offsets that can be detached after flowering in the spring, or by seed that germinates at 70°.

Potting: Use a 4- to 5-inch pot for bulbs that are up to 2 inches in diameter. Repotting is not required for several years, but top-dress with fresh soil at the beginning of each growing season.

Culture: Pot firmly in a rich fibrous loam with coarse sand added to give good drainage. Peatmoss may be incorporated in the soil if it is inclined to be on the clay side. Keep soil moderately moist until growth starts. Then, feed with liquid fertilizer every two weeks. Maintain a humid atmosphere and do not let the temperature drop lower than 50°. Shade during summer, but grow in full sunshine the remainder of the year. Rest bulbs after flowering by laying pots on sides. Let dry somewhat, but do not allow soil to get so dry that bulbs shrivel. A spray of water around the pots will keep the bulbs fresh.

Pests: Mealy bug.

CYTISUS CANARIENSIS (GENISTA)

Yellow Treasure for March

An evergreen shrub that flowers profusely with terminal clusters of bright yellow, pea-shaped blossoms. Young plants are easily and inexpensively procured. A few pots of this cytisus add a colorful touch over a long period in early or late spring.

Cool to moderate greenhouse: 45° to 55°F.

Propagation: By cuttings of young wood. These root easily any time at 70°, but are taken to best advantage in spring. They make small flowering plants the following March. Plants from seed sown in March reach flowering size in two years.

Potting: Transfer rooted cuttings to 3-inch pots. Spring cuttings will be ready for firm potting in 5's or 6's by late summer. Repot in 7's or 8's after spring flowering.

Culture: Grow in a light sandy loam, but do not add peatmoss since Cytisus likes a neutral soil and most peatmoss is acid. Pinch the ends of the strongest shoots several times to get well-branched shapely plants, taking the last pinch in December. Plunge pots in sand or cinders, and grow in full sun except when light shade is necessary to keep down temperature. Maintain high humidity and syringe daily until fall. Then set plants in the coolest spot in the greenhouse; buds will not form at temperatures above 60°. At 55°, plants will flower in March; at 45° as late as April.

Pests: Red spider and mealy bug.

DAPHNE

Fragrance for Early Winter

An evergreen shrub with wonderfully fragrant blooms in dense terminal clusters. D. odora has white to purple flowers; D. odora marginata (illustrated) is similar with white-edged leaves; those of D. Cneorum, the Rose Daphne, are pink. Plants can easily be forced into flower in early winter. Daphne is slow-growing, but specimens from 2 to 3 feet are possible.

Cool greenhouse: 45°F.

Propagation: By cuttings of young vigorous shoots that are produced early in spring after flowering. Remove any flower buds that may be present and root in sand and peatmoss or vermiculite at 55°.

Potting: Transfer young plants to small pots; then move to 5's or 6's, which will be sufficiently large for good-sized plants.

Culture: Good drainage is essential. Provide a compost of decayed manure or peatmoss and sandy loam in equal proportions. Soil should be slightly acid, but high in organic material. Care must be taken not to overwater, since these plants cannot stand a soggy condition at the roots. Feed with a solution of ammonium sulphate—1 teaspoon to 1 gallon of water—or with a complete fertilizer every two weeks from spring to fall while plants are making growth. Keep cool until the middle of December, then place in warmer spot at 50° to 55° for forcing. Plants will force in about eight weeks, or by the end of February with this treatment. They may be plunged outdoors in semi-shade during the summer.

Pests: Green fly, thrips, scale and leaf spot.

Desert Pea (See CLIANTHUS.)

DIETES

An Iris Oddity

A winter- and spring-flowering iris well suited to pot culture. Most of the blooms of this interesting plant last for only a day, but they are produced continually for several weeks. (*Hortus Second* lists it as Morea, but modern botany gives it a separate group.) Dietes has a hard rhizome, evergreen foliage, and a long wiry stem. A perennial, it flowers for several years, if faded blooms are *not* picked. Good varieties include: D. bicolor with stiff green foliage and beautiful yellow blooms brown spotted; D. iridiodes, a robust grower with waxy white flowers marked with yellow and blue; D. catenulata, low-growing, with fanlike foliage and white blooms having lavender styles and a yellow beard. A number of named varieties are available.

Cool to moderate greenhouse: 50° to 55°F.

Propagation: By division of rhizomes just as for bearded iris.

Potting: A small division requires a 6-inch pot. Shift as size increases.

Culture: Grow in sandy loam and give full sun. Soil should be kept moderately moist all the time. Provide a stake or the long wiry scape will fall over. Shade plants and keep as cool as possible during summer.

Pests: Scale.

DIMORPHOTHECA ECKLONIS CAPE MARIGOLD

Black-eyed Daisies on a Shrub

A shrubby perennial with large daisy-like flowers that open in the sun but close at night. Striking black centers and long thin white rays, purple streaked on the underside, make this a charming flower. Blooms come intermittently through the year, but in abundance during spring and summer. The plant grows 3 feet high and has an excellent spreading habit. It is useful for bedding outdoors in summer as well as for flowering in pots under glass. Other species are available.

Cool greenhouse: 45° to 50°F.

Propagation: By cuttings of half-ripened wood in early spring.

Potting: Pot three or four plants to a 5-inch pot. Transfer to larger pots in summer as required.

Culture: Dimorphotheca is of easy culture and does well in any rich loamy soil with a little coarse sand. Feed with liquid

Jasminum primulinum (Mesnyi), Primrose Jasmine, page 109-110.

Clivia miniata, Kafir Lily, page 68-69.

fertilizer every two weeks until flower buds develop; then once every three or four weeks as the plant matures and the pot becomes crowded with roots. Keep rather dry in winter but water well the rest of the year. Shade lightly during July and August, but at other times grow in full sunshine.

Pests: Mealy bug, red spider, and aphids.

EPISCIA

For Leaf Pattern and Bright Blooms

A trailing plant, beautiful for hanging baskets or pots. Flowers, opening through spring and summer, are small but numerous in white, scarlet, or purple. Foliage is soft and hairy, attractive all year. E. cupreata is slender and trailing with leaves marked by broad copper bands. E. coccinea has dark metallic green leaves and scarlet flowers.

Warm greenhouse: 65°F.

Propagation: By division of creeping roots, or cuttings rooted in peatmoss and sand, or vermiculite at any time. Transfer small plants to 3- or 4-inch pots in light fibrous soil.

Potting: Line wire baskets with an inch of sphagnum moss and fill with soil. Set one large or three small plants in an 8-inch basket for a quick show, or grow singly in 4- to 6-inch pots, depending on the size.

Culture: A warm house and dense humidity of about 80 percent is essential. This plant suffers at temperatures under 60°. Provide rich loam lightened with rotted manure and enough sand for free drainage. Water well through the summer, but give less water from October through February. Keep water off foliage to avoid mildew and botrytis. Shade during bright weather from March to October.

Pests: Mealy bug.

EUCHARIS AMAZON LILY

Beautiful White Scented Blooms

A bulbous plant that is a great favorite wherever grown. It bears clusters of sparkling fragrant white flowers on 12- to 18-inch stems. The large ovate leaves are also attractive. Eucharis usually flowers in the spring and summer, though it has no specific flowering time. As a rule, blooms come after alternate periods of growth and rest. This is definitely a warm greenhouse plant. It is useless to try it in a cool house, though I have carried mine through the winter successfully at 55° F. When in flower, the plant still wants warm conditions and should not be moved into a cool spot as you would most bulbous blooms. E. grandiflora (E. Amazonica), the species grown, is native of Colombia. Several suppliers carry it for delivery any time of the year.

Warm greenhouse: 60° to 65°F.

Propagation: Bulbs multiply readily under good conditions but like most evergreen bulbous plants, Eucharis suffers a setback if roots are disturbed. Make separations only when plants have grown too large for pots, or when additional plants are wanted. Do this when the bulb is matured and the plant resting. The simplest way to break bulbs apart is to soak them in water. Work the old soil loose with the fingers, and make divisions at the root joints with a sharp knife. Pot small bulbs in 3's, and keep growing on and shifting to larger-sized pots, as required. Seed germinates at a temperature of 65° to 70° and is best sown during January or February.

Potting: The bulbs you buy are a little more than 2 to 3 inches in diameter, so a 5-inch pot suits them well. Shift to pots three sizes larger when required. Good specimens in 10's or 12's are possible. Amazon lilies can also be grown directly in the soil of benches. The long-lasting flowers are excellent for bouquets.

Culture: Cover bulbs about half their depth and plant firmly, taking care not to injure roots. Use good coarse fibrous soil and peatmoss with sand to keep the mixture porous. Water sparingly until growth starts, but keep soil always moderately moist. Bulbs will root faster at a temperature of 70° to 80° with bottom heat. A closed case is excellent for this purpose. Light shading is needed during bright summer weather, but too dense shade will produce spindly growth, so give full sunshine from October to May.

With proper handling, strong plants can be brought into bloom two or three times a year, and there is no harm to bulbs. I have never succeeded in doing this but many of my friends have no trouble at all. A semi-rest period is needed to get the plant to flower each time. This is done by letting soil dry off gradually for 4 or 5 weeks after blooming, but do not let it become so arid that foliage dries. Water moderately when there are signs of wilting; water liberally after new shoots become visible. Feed with nitrate of soda or ammonium sulphate —1 teaspoon to 1 gallon of water—weak manure water, or any other complete liquid fertilizer that you use. Grow at 65° to 70° night temperature for best results. Never give less than 55°.

Pests: Thrips, green fly, and mealy bug.

EUCOMIS PINEAPPLE LILY

A Flower-Covered Pineapple

A bulb from the Cape of Good Hope with creamy white blooms on a thick, tight, flower spike. This emerges from bright green, strap-shaped leaves, and only about 10 inches of the upper part of the stalk bears flowers. A rosette of leaves similar to those on a pineapple terminates the spike. In June, E. punctata, which grows to 2 feet, has creamy white, star-shaped flowers. The foliage is dark green and mottled purple underneath. In March or April, E. undulata bears a dense flower head of bright green. The large brown leaves are undulated and shiny. E. pedunculata has a 10-inch flower head along an 18-inch stem. The numerous blooms in late spring are tubular at first; then they open wide in green or glistening white marked with purple. Foliage is dark green and erect. The crowning leaves are 2-inches across.

Cool greenhouse: 45° to 50°F.

Propagation: By offsets or seeds in the spring. Seed germinates quickly but it takes three years to produce flowering plants. Bulbs should be separated only when pots are crowded, since the plant is set back if roots are disturbed.

Potting: Bulbs, from more than 2 to 3 inches in diameter, are planted in 4- to 6-inch pots, depending on size. Repot or top-dress each spring, taking care not to disturb roots more than necessary.

Culture: Bulbs may look rather mutilated when you get them but don't let their condition bother you. They are joined solidly and do not separate well. They appear scarred when cut. This does no harm. Plant bulbs with the crown about 1 inch deep, and water moderately. Little or no additional water is required through the winter until late February, when soil should be moistened well as the plant starts into growth. Like all bulbs of the lily family, Eucomis requires a well-drained, fibrous soil. Leafmold or peatmoss may be added up to one-third if you have clay soil. Grow at a night temperature of 45° to 50°, and feed with a complete fertilizer every other week. Bulbs may be grown on in the same pots for three or four years.

Pests: Aphids and green fly.

Fame Flower (See TALINUM.)

FELICIA AMELLOIDES BLUE MARGUERITE

Wealth of Blue Daisies

A South African plant with exquisite sky-blue, daisies on long wiry stems. This is an old-time favorite that blooms in winter and makes an excellent pot plant, about 1 foot high.

Cool to moderate greenhouse: 50° to 55°F.

Propagation: By cuttings taken during May or June. These produce flowering plants the following winter.

Potting: Transfer rooted cuttings directly to 4-inch pots, then to 6's and 8's, before roots become pot-bound.

Culture: Felicia does well in good soil that is slightly acid, but wants a good supply of moisture at all times. Keep young plants growing steadily and feed with liquid manure, ammonium sulphate, or nitrate of soda—1 teaspoon to 1 gallon of water—once a week. Shade lightly during summer, and never grow cooler than 45° in winter. If growth becomes too lush, give less water.

Pests: Mealy bug, aphids, and thrips.

Ferraria (See IRIS FAMILY.)
Flame Flower (See PHLOGACANTHUS.)
Franciscea (See BRUNFELSIA.)

FRANCOA

Spikes of Spring White or Pink

An herbaceous plant from 1 to 3 feet high with dense, curved spikes of white or pink flowers in March or April. F. ramosa has the best branching habit with white flowers, 1-inch thick, on stems up to 2 feet; F. appendiculata is a pink variety.

Cool greenhouse: 40° to 50°F.

Propagation: By seed sown in sandy soil during February or March at 50°. This produces plants of flowering size the following spring. Divisions may be made at potting time. Start new plants every two or three years, since old ones do not flower well.

Potting: Set seedlings 2 inches apart in large pans or flats, where moisture is easily controlled. When they are 4 to 5 inches high, transfer plants singly to 4-inch pots; then on to 6's or 7's before they become pot bound. Plant divisions in 4 or 5-inch pots in late spring or fall.

Culture: Grow in loam and sand. Water well and feed every two weeks during spring and summer, but keep a little drier from fall to February, and feed only once or twice. Young plants do well if plunged in a cold frame during the summer. Pinch off first blooms from young plants, if large specimens are wanted.

Pests: Aphids.

FUCHSIA LADIES-EAR-DROPS

Victorian Favorites

A popular old-fashioned plant and one of the finest you can grow. While primarily spring- and summer-flowering, it can be kept in bloom through the winter, if you wish. Most of the fuchsias grown now are hybrids of F. fulgens and F. magellanica. Colors range from rose-red and purple to white. F. procumbens, with pale orange flowers, is an attractive trailing variety for hanging baskets. F. corymbiflora has deep red flowers about 4 inches long. It will grow to 6 feet and requires staking.

Warm greenhouse: 60°F.

Propagation: By 3- to 4-inch cuttings of wood on which flower buds have not yet formed. These root at 65° any time of year that soft growth can be taken. In fact, Fuchsias are one of the easiest plants to root. Start in January or February for plants that will flower the following spring or summer.

Potting: Plant singly in 3-inch pots, and shift to 4's or 5's before the root ball gets matted on the outside. Growth is stunted on plants that get pot-bound. When they are semi-dormant, replant in pots two or three sizes larger.

Culture: Grow in a fibrous soil of loam and peatmoss with a little sand added, if necessary, to provide drainage. Pinch to induce good branching and maintain a humid atmosphere. Carry on in the greenhouse or plant outside during the summer. Shade and support with stakes. Feeding with liquid fertilizer will prolong flowering. Use ammonium sulphate—1 teaspoon to 2 gallons of water—or any other fertilizer you like. Do not feed heavily at one time, however, or buds will drop. During fall, fuchsias have a natural resting period that lasts for about a month. At this time, cut back mature plants and repot in fresh soil. Specimens up to 10- or 12-inch pots can be grown this way, but the healthiest and best-looking are developed from new cuttings started each year.

Pests: Aphids, thrips, scale, and mealy bug.

GAZANIA (MERIDIANA)

Rich Color from May to Fall

A plant rarely found in home greenhouses but well worth growing for its wealth of yellow, orange, scarlet, and sometimes purple daisies. Plants bloom in May and continue through the summer. Gazania is a native of the Cape of Good Hope and one of the finest of the many small, tender perennials that come from that area. Flowers close at night. The orange G. splendens (illustrated) grows up to 1 foot. G. Pavonia, is orange-yellow; G. Pottsii, a pure yellow grows to 14 inches. There is also a white species, G. pygmaea, but I have not been able to find it. Excellent named varieties of wonderful size and color are available.

Cool greenhouse: 50°F.

Propagation: By cuttings in the spring from side shoots taken at the base of the plant, or seed, which germinates readily in January. Both flower the same year. Plants may also be increased by division of roots.

Potting: Transfer small plants to 3-inch pots, and then to 6's when well established. Plant divisions in 3- or 4-inch pots, depending on size of roots.

Culture: Use a rich fibrous loam with coarse sand added to provide good drainage. Soil should be disease-free, for gazania has soft roots subject to root rot. Do not add acid peatmoss; plants do best in neutral soil. In June, I set my plants out in the garden where they bloom most of the summer. Then in fall root clumps are divided and brought into the greenhouse for the winter.

Pests: White fly, aphids. Controls for mildew may also be needed.

Genista (See CYTISUS.)

GLADIOLUS TRISTIS AND BLANDUS

For Cut Flowers of Beauty and Fragrance

Bulbous plants that bloom from February to late spring. Flowers of G. tristis concolor are cream colored, resembling large freesias more than gladiolus, and appear three to five on a stem. Blooms are very fragrant, especially at night. Foliage is delicate, about 2 feet high, so staking is necessary. G. blandus has pink blooms.

Cool greenhouse: 50°F.

Propagation: By offsets, separated in fall.

Potting: Grow in a 5- to 8-inch bulb pan, depending on size of display wanted, or directly in bench soil about 2 inches apart.

Culture: Corms are available in fall and, if planted in November, bloom during February and March. Use a rich sandy loam, and plant about an inch apart, pressing them into the soil just as you would ixias. Water after planting. Additional water is not needed until growth starts. Set pots underneath a bench until growth appears; then place in full sun. After flowering, allow foliage to continue to grow; then in spring, set corms out in the garden, where they will rejuvenate themselves and may be forced again the next winter.

Pests: Aphids and thrips.

GLORIOSA GLORY LILY

Blaze of Color with a Climbing Lily

A climbing lily of dramatic beauty with brilliant coloring and wavy form. It blooms in early spring. The numerous crisp petal segments are crimped on the edges and curve abruptly back, making the long-spreading stamens prominent. Colors are in rich, melting tones of golden-orange to rose. G. Rothschildiana (illustrated), the most colorful and popular species, reaches 3 to 6 feet with numerous golden-crimson blooms, toned cream at the base. Blooms of G. superba, a 6 foot or higher species, open bright yellow and red, and change to deep scarlet. G. Plantii (virescens), growing to 3 or 4 feet, has bright red flowers. Several other good varieties are available.

Warm greenhouse: 60°F.

Propagation: By offsets from old tubers in fall. Remove these with care to avoid breaking brittle roots. The tubers may be cut into two sections if each has an eye. Bring into growth slowly with bottom heat. Seed takes two to three years to produce blooming-sized plants. Plant during February or March at 75°.

Potting: Long, slender tubers two or more years old are available in fall. Plant just below the surface in loose sandy soil that drains freely, one to a 6-inch pot, or three to an 8-inch pot.

Culture: Blooms in early March are possible by starting tubers in December or January. Water moderately and give bottom heat. Growth is slow at first, but rapid after shoots appear, when more water and a temperature of 60° are wanted. Plants respond readily to feeding, so apply a complete liquid fertilizer once every ten days until flowering. Then let foliage mature slowly. After leaves turn yellow, store tubers dry until the following fall.

Pests: Scale, bulb mite, and aphids.

Glory Bower or Glory Tree (See CLERODENDRON.)
Glory Bush (See TIBOUCHINA.)
Glory Lily (See GLORIOSA.)
Glory of The Sun (See LEUCOCORYNE.)
Glory Pea (See CLIANTHUS.)

Gloxinia (See SINNINGIA.)
Golden Hurricane Lily (See LYCORIS.)
Golden Spider Lily (See LYCORIS.)
Guernsey Lily (See NERINE.)

HAEMANTHUS BLOOD LILY

A Glowing Red Amaryllid

A spring- or fall-flowering amaryllid from South Africa. The bloom is borne on a single stout stalk about a foot high. Good bulbs produce bright red flowers up to 10 inches across. These form a sphere of 100 to 150 star-shaped flowers from which protrudes a pincushion of bright stamens. The luxuriant palmate or oval leaves, about 4 inches wide and up to 14 inches long, generally appear after the flower, but H. Katharinae, one of the most gorgeous reds, blooms in spring after foliage has developed. The red H. multiflorus, a commonly grown species, is usually spring flowering before foliage; the scarlet H. coccineus is fall flowering and also before foliage. Several other interesting species and hybrids are available.

Cool to warm greenhouse: 50° to 60°F.

Propagation: By offsets detached in spring, but Haemanthus multiplies slowly, which accounts for its high price.

Potting: Bulbs are 3 to 6 inches in diameter and require a pot about 2 inches larger. Top-dress with fresh soil at the beginning of each growing season. Repotting is necessary only once in three or four years. This is another bulb that is set back if roots are disturbed.

Culture: Pot firmly with the top of the bulb slightly protruding, in a rich, fibrous loam that drains readily. Bulbs are available from fall to spring and should be kept on the dry side when dormant. Water just enough to keep the bulb from shrinking. Start dormant bulbs slowly, but water well after growth appears, and feed every other week with weak liquid manure. H. multifloris is dormant during winter. H. Katharinae is practically evergreen and should not be dried off. My very large bulb of this variety produced an imperfect bloom from the side. I cut it off thinking that it would flower again but it did not produce another bloom until the next year. H. coccineus grows all winter but is dormant in summer. The plants like a humid atmosphere and daily syringing during hot weather. Shade lightly during summer, but at other times grow in full sun.

Pests: Green fly and red spider.

HARDENBERGIA

A Miniature Wisteria

An evergreen twiner with long racemes of small flowers. H. comptoniana is a bright blue-violet; H. monophylla, a rosy-violet. There is also a white variety, H. alba, but I do not find it available. The hardenbergias reach 12 to 15 feet. Yet they do not behave like the more vigorous climbers, but flower when quite small from winter to spring. This makes them especially well suited to the small greenhouse or lean-to.

Cool greenhouse: 50°F.

Propagation: By cuttings of new growth in March for plants that will flower the following year. Seed sown in February or March produces flowering plants in 12 to 18 months.

Potting: Transfer small plants or rooted cuttings to 3-inch pots. Plants started in spring require a 5- or 6-inch pot by summer or fall, and an 8-inch pot the following spring.

Culture: A well-drained loam with peatmoss and a little sand is suitable. Feed with a complete liquid fertilizer or liquid manure during the spring- and summer-growing season. Syringe daily in bright weather and shade from strong summer sun. A wire loop, bamboo canes, or any kind of trellis may be used to train the slender vines.

Pests: Aphids, red spider, mealy bug, and scale.

HEBE SPECIOSA (VERONICA SPECIOSA)

Violet Racemes in Midwinter

An evergreen shrub with violet flowers in 4-inch racemes. Hebe can usually be forced into bloom in midwinter. In pots, it flowers when quite small and rarely grows over 2 feet tall. A number of hybrids are available.

Cool to moderate greenhouse: 45° to 55°F.

Propagation: By cuttings of half-ripened wood. Taken during early spring, these produce small flowering plants the following year, and good-sized plants in two years.

Potting: Transfer to 3-inch pots when rooted.

Culture: Loam with peatmoss or leafmold suits this Hebe very well. Pinch growth as soon as it starts and again when shoots are a few inches long. Set plants outdoors during the summer. Lift and repot in early September, being careful not to break roots. Feed with a complete fertilizer or give two or three applications of liquid fertilizer two weeks apart. Start new plants every other year, since old ones become unsatisfactory unless they can be grown on in very large pots and allowed to develop long roots.

Pests: Aphids.

HIBISCUS ROSA-SINENSIS CHINA ROSE

Pastel Blooms in Summer

A flowering shrub suitable for the medium or large greenhouse where considerable space is available. Only hybrids of this one species that reaches 3 to 8 feet are grown. Flowers are white or in shades of soft pink, apricot, orange, yellow, and deep red, and both single and double. Blooms appear through summer and well into fall.

Warm greenhouse: 65°F.

Propagation: By 4-inch cuttings taken in spring. These root readily at 65°. Plant in sand and peatmoss, preferably in a closed case where humidity can be controlled.

Potting: Transfer rooted cuttings to 3-inch pots, and shift to 4's before they become root-bound. Transfer up to 10's, 12's or larger pots as required. Top-dress or repot in February.

Culture: Use a sandy soil that is well drained or straight peatmoss. Culture is comparatively easy in a warm humid greenhouse. The earlier plants are started in spring, the sooner they will flower. Feed every ten days with manure water or a complete liquid fertilizer. Pinch shoots to induce bushiness, and grow in shade through spring and summer. After flowering, plants may be trimmed hard to keep them in shape and under control. Best results are obtained with young plants from two-to-four-years old; if you grow older plants, top-dress them after flowering, taking care not to disturb roots.

Pests: Scale, mealy bug, and green fly.

HOLMSKIOLDIA CHINESE HAT PLANT

Orange-Red for Fall

A flowering shrub effective as a large pot plant with willowy evergreen stems and orange-to-red flowers that look like verbenas. They are showy and unusual in late fall. Only one species, H. sanguinea, is grown under glass.

Warm greenhouse: 60°F.

Propagation: By cuttings of half-mature wood in early spring. They root easily at 70° in peatmoss or sand.

Potting: Transfer rooted cuttings to small pots and on to 5's or 6's before they become pot-bound. Continue to shift to larger pots as required, up to 8's, 10's, or larger.

Culture: Plants thrive in any light porous soil and must be watered frequently during the growing season. Mulch with peatmoss to hold moisture. Syringe daily during spring and summer until flower buds show color. Full sun at all times is essential to flowering. Plants may be grown on in the same pots for several years if top-dressed every February.

Pests: Aphids, scale, and mealy bug.

Plumbago capensis, Leadwort, page 134-135.

TOP LEFT: *Vriesia carinata*, page 51-55. TOP RIGHT: *Veltheimia viridifolia*, page 170-171. BOTTOM LEFT: *Eucomis undulata*, Pineapple Lily, page 82-83. BOTTOM RIGHT: *Aechmea fulgens discolor*, page 51-55.

HOYA CARNOSA WAX PLANT

Fragrant Waxy Flowers on a Small Climber

An evergreen climber with loose waxen clusters of bloom on trailing stems that extend from the axils of smooth fleshy leaves. H. carnosa reaches 6 to 8 feet under good conditions, but it is easily kept within bounds. The delicate, fragrant white blooms tinted pink, and with deep pink centers, come in late spring and summer. H. bella is a white, summer-flowering, hanging-basket type, and requires a warm greenhouse (60° to 70°F).

Moderate to warm greenhouse: 55° to 60°F.

Propagation: By cuttings taken from terminal growth in spring and rooted in sand and peatmoss, or in vermiculite. Give plenty of humidity and a 70° bottom heat. An easier method of reproduction is by layering. Fasten a joint of a branch with roots on it in a pot of sphagnum moss or peatmoss. Cut off the branch from the parent when the new plant is established.

Potting: Transfer rooted cuttings to 4-inch pots, then shift to 6's. Be sure they have plenty of root room. Larger specimens may require a pot up to 8 or 10 inches. Plants may be grown in the same pot for several years. Top-dressing with fresh soil is beneficial when the new season's growth begins.

Culture: Grow in loose fibrous soil, adding coarse sand as necessary to keep the mixture light and loose. Hoya will not tolerate wet or stagnant conditions at the roots. The plant rests or is semi-dormant during the winter and makes little growth until the longer, warmer days of spring. It wants plenty of ventilation through the year and all sunlight possible, except from June through August, when partial shade is essential. Syringe foliage until flower buds appear. Syringing after that time might cause the tender buds to drop. Wires or long canes are needed for growing the plant up the side and across the roof of the greenhouse. Flowers appear on spurs from the axils of leaves. Don't cut these off or plants will not bloom again, until new spurs have had time to develop.

Pests: Mealy bug.

Hyalis (See Ixia.)
Hymenocallis (See Ismene.)

IBOZA RIPARIA (MOSCHOSMA RIPARIUM)

A White-flowering Christmas Tree

A pyramidal shrub covered with tiny, creamy white, black-anthered flowers from December until February. It is especially handsome for the Christmas holidays.

Warm greenhouse: 60°F.

Propagation: By seed sown in March, or from 3-to-4-inch cuttings which produce flowering plants the same year. Cuttings root readily in a closed case at 55° to 60°. Put new young plants in 3's, and let them continue at this temperature until well established. Since this plant grows quite large, only one or two would be wanted in a small greenhouse.

Potting: Transfer to 6's or 7's before small pots become filled with roots and plants are starved. Pot firmly. During March, repot plants to be carried on a second year in 8's or 9's.

Culture: Iboza does well in a fibrous loam such as you would use for chrysanthemums, but add some well-rotted manure so the roots will have something to feed on over a long period. Grow in full sun and water freely while in active growth, but moderately after October. Syringe foliage on the hot days of July and August. After the plant has matured and the pot is filled with roots, feed with liquid fertilizer every ten days. Pinch growth once or twice in the early stages to make a well-branched small specimen or let go without pinching for a shapely plant up to 3 or 4 feet. Prune after flowering and grow in the sunshine so good growth will form to provide cuttings to root the following year. If the plant is in good condition, it may be grown on a second year, but shake off the old soil and repot in fresh during March.

Pests: Aphids, red spider, and mealy bug.

Ifafa Lily (See CYRTANTHUS.)

INCARVILLEA

Colorful Bouquets and Ferny Foliage

An evergreen plant with small but numerous tubular flowers in terminal clusters of cream, blush pink, purple, red, or yellow. Blooms appear on stems 1 to 2 feet high, rising from handsome, fernlike, basal foliage. Flowering starts in early spring and continues through October. I. Delavayi has rose-purple flowers; I. grandiflora is similar but rose-red; I. Olgae (illustrated) has pale pink flowers, and I. variabilis, a vigorous grower, has pale rose flowers. Others are available.

Cool greenhouse: 45° to 50°F.

Propagation: By seed that germinates rapidly in the spring; and by division or cuttings in fall. Cuttings taken from young growth just above the base, root readily in a mixture of sand and peatmoss, or in vermiculite.

Potting: Transfer young plants to 3-inch pots and on up to 6's or 7's before pots become filled with roots. Plant divisions in 4-to-7-inch pots, depending on size. When planted in benches, space 10 inches apart.

Culture: Incarvillea does well in a light sandy soil. Partial shading is necessary in summer, but grow in full sun the rest of the year. If desired, set outdoors during the summer in a protected spot, but lift and divide root clumps in early September. Pot these or grow as a bench crop in the greenhouse. Keep on the dry side from October to February. After growth starts in February, feed with ammonium sulphate or nitrate of soda—1 teaspoon to 1 gallon of water—every ten days until flower buds appear.

Pests: White fly, aphids, and thrips.

India-Hawthorn (See RAPHIOLEPIS.)
Iris (See IRIS FAMILY.)

IRIS FAMILY

For Curiosity and Pleasure

In addition to Babiana and Ixia, there are a number of oddities in the iris family that are a lot of fun to grow—some for unique form, flowers, and habit; others for ineffable beauty of bloom.

I was quite successful in bringing a group into flower and have others of fair promise. Iris Susiana especially made a glorious display, and I felt well repaid for the trouble and expense, even though I lost the plant after one season of bloom. This often happens with such plants in the home greenhouse when you are too busy to do all the things you should at the proper time.

The Iris that are discussed here are for the *cool to moderate greenhouse* (50° to 55°F.), and all take the same treatment if blooms are wanted from late winter to early spring.

Propagation: By division of root stock or offsets in fall at repotting time, or by seed sown in spring.

Potting: Use a 4-to-6-inch pot, depending on size of rootstock, corm, or bulb, and pot rather firmly with top just below the surface of the soil. Large rhizomes, corms, or bulbs are planted singly. Small ones are set five or six to a deep 6-inch pot. Repot in fresh soil every fall.

Culture: Dormant rhizomes, tubers, corms, or bulbs for these plants are available from August to November. Plant in a porous sandy loam that water will run through readily. The condition of soil moisture is the key to success. Water moderately after planting in fall. Then water freely as growth starts. If soil is permitted to dry out just once during the growing period, "blindness" will result. Two or three feedings with a complete liquid fertilizer about three weeks apart are beneficial. Do not give night temperature of more than 50° to 55°, or flowers may blast. After flowering is over, dry the foliage off gradually by withholding water until the soil becomes bone dry. Store pots where soil can remain dry until the following fall, or remove bulbs or root stock and store in dry sand or sphagnum moss. This is important. Some gardeners even place a pane of glass over the pot to make sure no water will reach the soil.

Pests: Scale and thrips.

CYPELLA

I find available two varieties of this odd plant. C. Herbertii with plaited leaves bears from a scape one to three yellow flowers about 3 inches across. C. plumbea has blue flowers that last but a few hours. They are desirable for their unique form.

FERRARIA UNDULATA

This unusual dwarf iris comes from South Africa. It is very closely related to tigridia, but much better for greenhouse forcing. The flowers are huge on stems 8 to 12 inches high above narrow wavy leaves. They appear from inflated sheaths similar to orchids. I had difficulty in locating a source for the rhizomes, at first, but a most cooperative bulb importer came to the rescue. You will find many suppliers most helpful in this for they are always interested in the rarer plants themselves and always glad for new material to add to their line.

IRIS BUCHARICA

Here is a handsome, worth-while iris for the greenhouse—one that should be included in any collection. It gives you five to seven bright yellow flowers with a wavy crest on a stalk about 1 foot high. You will find it wants a little more water than the others.

IRIS SUSIANA

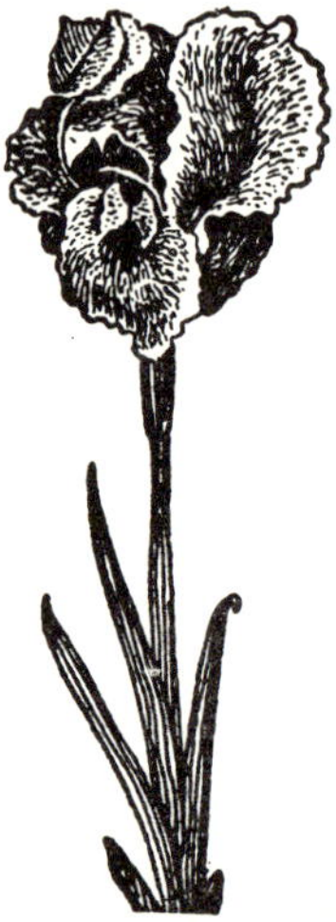

This most beautiful member of the group has narrow foliage 6 to 9 inches long and a tremendous single flower on a 12-inch stem. The background color is a silvery gray marked with heavy veins and dots of a deep purple-black. The beard of both the upright and falling petals is a deep bronze, and in the center of each falling petal is a large black spot. Rhizomes are available from October to December and, while quite expensive, are well worth any price you have to pay. Be sure to try Iris Susiana for a grand treat in early spring, but remember, after flowering the rhizomes must be stored bone dry.

MOREA

Flowers of this interesting iris last just a day, but blooms are produced in quick succession. Good varieties include: M. edulis with a long, wiry, solitary leaf and lilac flowers spotted with yellow; M. polystacha, taller with lilac flowers having a large yellow spot at the base. M. ramosissima has basal leaves and bright yellow flowers in clusters that last for several weeks. Plants will bloom during the winter or spring. (See also DIETES.)

SPARAXIS *WAND-FLOWER*

These are free-flowering plants with large, brilliant funnel-shaped flowers on wiry stems. Leaves are basal, 6 to 20 inches long. Blends in lavender, lilac, cream, yellow, salmon, scarlet, and orange are available. S. grandiflora is purple. S. tricolor is similar, except that flowers come in a wide variety of colors and are characterized by a yellow throat.

STREPTANTHERA CUPREA

This interesting oddity has copper-yellow flowers with purple throats edged black, and with a yellow spot in the center. It blooms in February or March, earlier than most of the group. Basal leaves develop in a fan about 4 inches long.

SYNNOTIA METELERKAMPIAE

Nine to twelve dark violet flowers grow on a 10-inch spike above broad leaves in a basal rosette. A worth-while plant.

TRITONIA (MONTBRETIA)

This half-hardy, cormous, lance-leaved plant bears several funnel-shaped flowers on each slender stem. Mixed blends in salmon, rose, orange, and scarlet are available. T. crocata has orange-red flowers in a loose, one-sided raceme; T. deusta is similar but blooms have a purple-black blotch.

WATSONIA (MERIANA)

One of the most popular of the group is this tall, vigorous, lance-leaved grower with gladiolus blooms on stiff erect stems.

W. angusta bears from twelve to twenty scarlet flowers. Flowers of W. longifolia are pale pink to deep rose; W. marginata is fragrant with rose-red blooms; and W. Wilmaniae is purplish-rose. Some watsonias are evergreen and are not dried off, but treated as green plants in the manner of Dietes. Your supplier will send you directions for handling them.

ISMENE (HYMENOCALLIS) — SEA DAFFODIL OR SPIDER LILY

Attractive Form and Exquisite Scent

An interesting amaryllid with fragrant blooms borne in an umbel on a stout leafless stem about 2 feet long. Most varieties flower in spring and summer, but one or two are winter blooming. I. caribaea has long shiny leaves and fragrant white flowers in winter. The fragrant I. occidentalis bears white flowers and is spring-flowering. Several named varieties are also available. Sulphur Queen has light yellow blooms of rare beauty. I. festalis is pure white, and is considered by many to be the most beautiful white in the amaryllis family.

Warm greenhouse: 60°F.

Propagation: By offsets, separated when bulbs are dormant. Seed germinates readily but two to three years are required to produce blooming-sized plants.

Potting: Small bulbs will take a 5-inch pot, larger ones a 7-inch. Repot in fresh soil before each growing season.

Culture: Plant in sandy loam with one-third peat or leafmold added. Ismene must have an acid soil for nutrients to be available. In alkaline soils, foliage turns yellow and growth is poor. During summer growth, always keep soil moist. Shade only lightly during the brightest weather, since this plant requires plenty of sunshine. Feed every ten days with ammonium sulphate—1 teaspoon to 1 gallon of water. Rest bulbs after foliage has fully matured, letting the soil become dry. Never grow cooler than 60°. Blooms by March or April are possible with repotting and watering in February.

Pests: Aphids, thrips, red spider, scale, and mealy bug.

IXIA (HYALIS)

Range of Delicate Colors

A charming cormous plant producing slender spikes 2 feet high with small, showy, funnel-shaped flowers above grassy leaves. Colors range from white to pink, red, lilac, and yellow. Ixias can be had in bloom from February on. I. maculata is yellow; I. viridiflora is pale green with a black throat and very interesting; I. campanulata (I. speciosa, I. crateroides) is 1 foot high with dark crimson flowers; I. leucantha grows to 2 feet with white blossoms. Many named hybrids are available and widely grown.

Cool greenhouse: 45° to 50°F.

Propagation: By offsets or seed. Offsets are separated in the fall. Seed sown in February or March will produce flowering-sized bulbs the third year.

Potting: Bulbs are comparatively small. Five or six are planted in a 5-inch pot.

Culture: Ixias are easy to flower well, if you don't try to force them too fast. You can plant them from the middle of September to October; the earlier, the better the bloom. Place pans in a cold frame and protect with 8 to 10 inches of straw until

December. The object is to get good stocky root growth. If bulbs are forced before this develops, foliage tends to stretch out and flowers are poor. Only one watering is needed till growth starts, but water freely thereafter. Plants may be set in full sun in the greenhouse, where they will flower from four to six weeks. Stake and tie foliage to develop trim-looking plants. After flowering, bulbs may be stored dry in the same pot they grew in until the following August. Then repot and force again.

Pests: Aphids and thrips.

IXORA

An Outstanding Greenhouse Shrub

A tropical shrub and one of the most suitable of woody evergreens for the large or small greenhouse. The plant has a good bushy habit and is very handsome as either a large or small-flowering pot plant. Blooms start in April or May and continue for a long period. They are among the showiest in the warm greenhouse. Flowers appear in dense, wide-spreading clusters from deep red through all shades of scarlet and orange to white. Suitable varieties for culture under glass include: I. coccinea, which has rose-to-scarlet blooms; I. Stricta Rubra with orange-red flowers; I. parviflora with fragrant white blooms; and I. macrothyrsa, one of the best, with large trusses of deep red flowers and long leaves.

Warm greenhouse: 60°F.

Propagation: From cuttings of half-ripened wood taken with four pairs of leaves and rooted in a mixture of sand and peatmoss, or in vermiculite, at 70°. They root easily at any time of year, but are best taken in spring.

Potting: Transfer rooted cuttings to 6-inch pots and give a temperature of 60° to 65°. Always pot firmly. Shift to larger pots and do not permit plants to become pot bound until they are of desired flowering size. Top-dress or repot with fresh soil in fall.

Culture: Ixoras are of relatively easy culture and available as pot plants from several suppliers. Grow in a soil of loose texture that drains well. Peatmoss and sand can be added, if necessary. High humidity during the spring- and summer-growing season is essential. Young plants do best if plunged in sand or cinders, which maintain an even moisture through the root ball. Give partial shade in summer, but grow in full sunshine the rest of the year. This plant will stand a tremendous amount of summer heat if given humidity with plenty of moisture, so syringe and water daily. Mature plants can be grown on in the same pots for three or four years if fed every ten days with liquid fertilizer. After flowering, prune back plants to about 2 joints. Leave on the best side shoots to give good form.

Pests: Brown scale and mealy bug.

JACOBINIA

A Rosy Glow of Tubular Flowers

An herbaceous evergreen especially desirable as a small or large winter-through-summer flowering pot plant. Blooms are showy in dense terminal heads with tubular flowers from crimson to purple, or yellow to orange. J. carnea, one of the most popular, is a strong grower with rose-purple blooms on stems almost a foot high. Plants may reach 4 feet if not restricted. J. coccinea (illustrated) is an erect grower with crimson flowers on a dense terminal spike; J. velutina has pink-to-crimson flowers in a short, dense, terminal inflorescence; J. Ghiesbreghtiana, (Justicia Ghiesbreghtiana) one of the best winter bloomers, has orange-crimson flowers.

Moderate to warm greenhouse: 55° to 60°F.

Propagation: By cuttings taken from old plants during April and rooted in sand or vermiculite at 55° to 60°.

Potting: Transfer cuttings to small pots and shift to 5's or 6's before they become crowded with roots. In fall repot plants to be grown on the second or third year in 8's or 10's.

Culture: Handle like Fuchsias (which see) for best results, and start new plants each season. Older plants can be grown on for several years, but get straggly if neglected. Grow in a loose fibrous soil with peatmoss, or peatmoss with sand, to provide good drainage. Jacobinia needs plenty of water and should never be permitted to become dry during the growing season. Pinch periodically to induce bushiness. Shade during spring and summer, but grow in full sun the rest of the year. Large plants in pots filled with roots require a liquid-fertilizer feeding every two weeks.

Pests: Aphids and red spider.

JASMINUM

Fragrant White Stars for Spring

Shrubby and semi-climbing plants suitable for small or large pots, if kept under control. Blooms are showy in clusters of white or yellow. They are especially popular with home gardeners who enjoy perfumed plants. Flowers appear in spring or summer. J. officinale is a climber with fragrant white blooms that are especially attractive. The variety grandiflorum is a bushy shrub known as the Royal or White Spanish Jasmine. It is one of the best whites with large showy blooms. J. Sambac is a fragrant, double white twiner in bloom almost all year. J. nudiflorum is a bushy grower with yellow flowers; J. primulinum (J. Mesnyi) is similar with semi-double yellow flowers and larger leaves.

Cool to warm greenhouse: 50° to 60°F.

Propagation: By cuttings best taken in spring when terminal shoots of half-ripened wood are 3 inches long. Root in sand, or peatmoss and sand, or in vermiculite at 70°

Potting: Transfer cuttings to 3-inch pots within four weeks, then on to 6's, when pots become fairly filled with roots. Take care not to overpot, since Jasmines do not like soggy conditions at the roots. Move to 8's or 10's when ready.

Culture: Jasmine is easy to grow and does well in a loose fibrous soil. Feed with a complete liquid fertilizer or manure water every two weeks during the growing season to encourage good growth and flowering. Syringe daily during warm weather, and grow in partial shade from spring to fall, but give full sunshine the rest of the year. Plants may be grown in the same pots for several years if fed regularly.

Pests: Aphids, thrips, red spider, mealy bug, and scale.

Kafir Lily (See SCHIZOSTYLIS.)

KALANCHOE UNIFLORA (KITCHINGIA UNIFLORA OR BRYOPHYLLUM UNIFLORUM)

For Bright Long-lasting Bloom

A good succulent for hanging pots or baskets, with slender stems that grow rapidly and soon reach down the side of the container. Numerous urn-shaped flowers appear in March. They are large for the size of the plant, about three-quarters of an inch long, and of an unusual translucent salmon-pink. Foliage resembles that of sedum.

Cool greenhouse: 50°F.

Propagation: By cuttings of jointed stems that root easily any time. Even single leaves may be used.

Potting: Plant 4 or 5 rooted cuttings in an 8-inch hanging pot or wire basket lined with an inch of sphagnum moss. Plants may be grown in the same containers for several years.

Culture: Grow in full sunshine all the time except for just a little shade in the hottest summer weather. Water in moderation all year round, but never let soil get dry. Plants should

Agapanthus africanus, Lily-of-the-Nile, page 33-34.

Nerine sarniensis, Guernsey Lily, page 122-124.

not be syringed overhead, since rot may develop. Grow in rich porous soil composed of decayed sod manure with a little coarse sand added to make it drain freely. Feed with a complete liquid fertilizer or nitrate of soda—1 teaspoon to 1 gallon of water—every two weeks from spring until fall.

Pests: Mealy bug. Stem rot develops under soggy conditions of soil. Do not use DDT on this plant.

Kangaroo Paw (See ANIGOZANTHUS.)
Kitchingia (See KALANCHOE.)

LACHENALIA CAPE COWSLIP

Midwinter Bells of Bloom

A bulb from the Cape of Good Hope with pink-to-red, yellow-to-orange, cream-to-blue, and violet flowers. In January and February the bells appear in tiers along a scape about 9 inches long. There are both erect and pendulous varieties, the latter are excellent for hanging baskets or pans. Since plants and flowers are small, you should plan to put in a hundred or more to make a splash of color that will last six or seven weeks. L. tricolor varieties are the most popular of the uprights, especially Nelsonii (illustrated). For drooping plants, species of L. pendula, are desirable. Some Lachenalias in the trade have whitish green flowers and do not amount to much, so take care in making selections.

Cool greenhouse: 50°F.

Propagation: By offsets that multiply readily and are divided in the fall. As many as a third of the new offsets from well-ripened plants will flower the following year. The rest can be planted for bloom the year after. Some home gardeners plant offsets in a row along the unused outside edge of a bench, near the glass where they are perfectly happy, yet out of the way. Seed sown in the fall germinates in about two weeks, and if well handled, will flower in late winter.

Potting: Use 5-inch or larger bulb pans or wire baskets. Fill the bulb pan with soil and push the bulbs down into it about half an inch deep and an inch apart. Line wire baskets with an inch of sphagnum moss and fill with soil. I always press some of the bulbs through the moss into the soil, so that they will grow out through the sides of the basket and give a well-rounded effect.

Culture: Plant bulbs in August or September, and grow in a rich, loose, fibrous loam, such as composted sod and manure, with up to one-fifth coarse sand for drainage. Water after planting to settle the soil, and set in a cold frame to make growth until November or December. Once growth starts, feed with liquid fertilizer two or three times. Protect from frost. A slight nip, however, will not do any harm. Water sparingly after bringing into the greenhouse until growth starts. Maintain a night temperature of not more than 50°. Lachenalias will not take forcing at high temperatures until after the flower scape appears. They can then be forced for a short time at 55° to 60°, if you want them for a special occasion. Stunted and malformed growth is certain if heat is too high in the beginning. Give all sunshine possible and admit fresh air when outdoor conditions are favorable, but, as with most other plants you grow under glass, avoid drafts. After flowering is past, keep foliage growing in sunshine to ripen bulbs fully. When leaves die back, store bulbs in the same pots and soil in which they grew until the following August; then remove and replant in fresh soil.

Pests: Green fly.

Ladies-Ear-Drops (See FUCHSIA.)
Lady-Of-The-Night (See BRUNFELSIA.)

LAPEIROUSIA (ANOMATHECA)

Red and Blue for Late Winter

A bulbous African plant with red or blue flowers from late winter to early spring. This is interesting to try even though it will never be as popular as the freesia, which it resembles, since it blooms later and lacks the fragrance. L. cruenta bears bright rosy-red flowers on one side of a foot-high spike. L. fissifolia is violet or white with a spike about 2 feet long. You will find this plant listed in catalogs as Anomatheca.

Cool greenhouse: 45°F.

Propagation: By offsets that increase rapidly. Separate into patches of three or more and not as single bulbs. Plant five or six to a pot.

Potting: Set about an inch and a half apart in a 5-inch or larger bulb pan. Transfer to larger sizes when pots become filled with roots, but do not disturb the earth ball. Repot each fall.

Culture: Plant in August to November in a light fibrous soil that drains well. Place in a cold frame, and keep pots covered with a layer of sand and 8 to 10 inches of straw until January first. Staking will be required to support foliage and blooms. After flowering let foliage mature fully to insure another crop of blooms the following year.

Pests: Aphids and thrips.

Lasiandra (See TIBOUCHINA.)
Leadwort (See PLUMBAGO.)

LEUCOCORYNE GLORY OF THE SUN

Sweet-scented Blue Stars

A worth-while winter-flowering bulbous plant from Chile. Bulbs are inexpensive, easily found, and make an intriguing show with umbels of fragrant, light blue, starry flowers. They have white centers and pronounced yellow anthers and are borne on long wiry stems above grassy basal foliage.

Cool to moderate greenhouse: 50° to 55°F.

Culture: Treat the same as Ixia (which see).

Lily Thorn (See CATESBAEA.)

LINARIA TRIORNITHOPHORA — THREE BIRDS FLYING

A Long-Spurred Violet "Snapdragon"

A small shrub with irregular blooms of violet and purple, striped orange. They appear in groups of three, hence the popular name. Well-established, 2- to 3-foot plants flower practically all year. In fact, Linaria is as nearly everblooming as any plant I know. This perennial from Spain and Portugal is another of those fine shrubs for the beginner. It is not fussy and seems to do well under almost any condition. Growth is fast and flowering-sized plants from either seed or cuttings are possible in a short time.

Moderate greenhouse: 55°F.

Propagation: By division during February or March for plants that flower by summer. Seed sown in spring will produce flowering plants by fall.

Potting: Grow two to three plants in a 6-inch pot.

Culture: Linaria does well in practically any soil and no special attention is required. Pinch to induce bushiness and grow in partial shade during late spring and summer.

Pests: I have never seen any insects bother this plant.

LOTUS BERTHELOTII

Red Clusters and Silver Foliage

An evergreen shrub excellent for hanging baskets with silver-gray foliage that streams down 4 to 5 feet. In beautiful contrast are the small clusters of bright red, pea-like flowers appearing in February and March. This is one of the most attractive and worth-while plants you can grow. Variety L. B. atrococcineus and Berthelotii are similar but the former has darker scarlet blooms with a black spot.

Cool to moderate greenhouse: 45° to 55°F.

Propagation: By division in February or March, or from cuttings in late spring. These root at 55° to 65°.

Potting: Transfer rooted cuttings to small pots, and then to 8-inch hanging baskets lined with an inch of sphagnum moss. Plant divisions directly in 8-inch baskets.

Culture: This plant is of easy culture and does well in any good soil. Water sparingly during the winter, but moderately during spring and summer. Feed once a week with a complete liquid fertilizer from the time plant starts into growth until the end of the flowering period. Place in full sunshine except during the hottest weather, when light shade is needed.

Pests: Red spider.

LUCULIA

Pink Flowers for Christmas

Clusters of deliciously sweet blooms in white, pink, and rose on a tender evergreen. The individual flowers look much like those of phlox, having a narrow tube flattened at the end, but about an inch and a half across. Luculia is one of the most beautiful flowering shrubs to bloom during late fall and winter. It must be grown to a large sized plant to be at its finest, but will flower in small pots. L. gratissima is the best variety; it reaches 8 to 10 feet and gives a mass of gorgeous pink flowers.

Moderate to warm greenhouse: 55° to 60°F.

Propagation: By ripened wood taken after flowering and rooted in sand and peatmoss, or in vermiculite at 70°. Harden plants off gradually to acclimate them to the lower temperature of the moderate-to-warm greenhouse.

Potting: Transfer rooted cuttings to 4-inch pots, then on to larger pots, before the first ones become filled with roots. Firm potting is essential to this vigorous grower. Repot in March if necessary.

Culture: Luculia is easy to grow and does well in a compost of equal parts fibrous loam and peatmoss with sand added, if necessary, for drainage. Young plants can be carried outdoors in summer in semi-shade with pots plunged to hold in moisture. Never allow plants to dry off. Feed with ammonium sulphate or nitrate of soda—1 teaspoon to 1 gallon of water. Apply either in place of water about once a week until flower buds appear. Pinch off young shoots until June or July. Move plants into the greenhouse by the end of August, for they will not set buds at a low temperature. After they have flowered, trim plants into an attractive shape and give less water.

Pests: Red spider and aphids.

LYCORIS — GOLDEN SPIDER OR GOLDEN HURRICANE LILY

Brilliance from the Orient

An amaryllid from China and Japan with large, orange-colored flowers on a stalk 1 to 3 feet long. Lycoris is one of the most striking plants you can grow under glass. The blooms measure 3 to 4 inches across and four to twelve are clustered on each stem. They appear in late fall or winter just as leaf growth develops. In spring, leaves turn yellow and die off. L. aurea is handsome, and the only variety available.

Cool to moderate greenhouse: 50° to 55°F.

Propagation: By offsets separated when the bulb is dormant.

Potting: Plant singly in 6- or 7-inch pots, depending on size of bulb. Repot only when necessary, taking care to preserve all the live roots possible. Bulbs are best left undisturbed in the same pot for several years.

Culture: Set bulbs in loose, rich, fibrous soil with the nose protruding above the surface. Do not add acid peatmoss since

Lycoris wants a neutral soil. Bulbs are dormant most of the summer, so start them into growth slowly. Feed with nitrate of soda—1 teaspoon to 1 gallon of water—to encourage vigorous foliage and quantity of bloom. Give full sunshine, except during the hot summer, when partial shade is needed.

Pests: Aphids, thrips, mealy bug, and scale.

Lygistum (See MANETTIA.)
Madagascar Jasmine (See STEPHANOTIS.)

MALVAVISCUS ARBOREUS (ACHANIA)

Scarlet for Winter and Summer

A shrubby plant with showy scarlet flowers resembling Abutilon, the flowering maple, but the blooms of Malvaviscus never fully open. It blooms both winter and summer, and flowers stay perfect for a long time. Several varieties of M. arboreus, that make 2-to-4 foot plants when pot grown, are available from southern suppliers. M. grandiflorus is vigorous and used for hedges in the South.

Warm greenhouse: 60°F.

Propagation: From side shoots taken during February and rooted in a closed propagating case at a temperature of 70° to 75°.

Potting: Transfer rooted cuttings to small pots and then directly to 6's. Each year after flowering is over, repot to 2 sizes larger until 12-inch pots are used.

Culture: Provide a mixture of equal parts peatmoss and fibrous loam with sand added for drainage. Grow in full sunshine, except during hottest spring and summer weather, when a light shade is needed. Feed every seven to ten days with ammonium sulphate—1 teaspoon to 1 gallon of water—or with liquid fertilizer. Keep soil very moist from spring to fall but moderately so during winter. After flowering is over, cut plants well back, since flowers appear on new wood. Plants plunged outdoors during summer will continue to bloom.

Pests: This plant is not subject to insects of any kind. The white grains that may appear on leaves are the plant's own waxy secretion.

MANETTIA BI-COLOR (LYGISTUM)

An Old-fashioned Easy-to-grow Vine

A twining plant up to 4 or 5 feet that blooms continuously with bright red, tube-shaped flowers tipped yellow. Flowers are short-lived but appear profusely.

Warm greenhouse: 60°F.

Propagation: By cuttings easily rooted at 60° to 65° in sand or peatmoss.

Potting: Plant in 3-inch pots. Cuttings taken in spring should be ready for 7's or 8's by June. Shift up to 10's or 12's, if such large plants are desired.

Culture: Provide a soil mixture of two parts fibrous loam and one part leafmold with coarse sand added for drainage. Pinch terminal growth to induce side branching. From June till the middle of September, plants may be grown in the greenhouse or plunged out in the garden. Syringe with water under pressure at least two or three times a week. Grow on the north or west side of the house where foliage will not cast heavy shade on other plants. Supply a trellis or train on bamboo stakes.

Pests: Red spider, aphids, and mealy bug.

Meriana (See WATSONIA.)
Meridiana (See GAZANIA.)
Mexican Orange-Flower (See CHOISYA.)
Mexican Star (See MILLA.)

MILLA BIFLORA — MEXICAN STAR

Fragrant Lilies to Cut

One of the best small-flowering bulbs of the lily family, with waxy white, fragrant flowers in winter or early spring. Blooms, usually two to five on 18-inch stems, are two and a half inches across and excellent for cutting. Each bulb produces a number of flower stalks. Foliage is short and grassy.

Cool greenhouse: 50°F.

Culture: Treat the same as Ornithogalum (which see).

Montbretia (See TRITONIA.)
Morea (See IRIS FAMILY.)
Moschosma (See IBOZA.)

NAEGELIA SMITHIANTHA

For Foliage as well as Flower

A tropical plant of the same family as the gloxinia and African violet with soft, heart-shaped leaves and terminal racemes of brilliant tubular flowers almost 2 inches long. It makes a good 5- or 6-inch pot plant for summer flowering. Available varieties include: N. zebrina (illustrated) with flowers spotted red and yellow and leaves veined purple-red, and Golden King with yellow flowers.

Warm greenhouse: 60°F.

Propagation: By offsets or trailing runners that root easily.

Culture: Treat the same as Sinningia (which see.)

NERINE GUERNSEY LILY

Scarlet Brilliance in Autumn

A very showy amaryllid. Flowers, appearing on leafless stems 1 to 2 feet high, are gay with re-curved petals and long bright stamens. September to November is flowering time for most varieties. Leaves are strap-shaped and appear after flowers have passed. N. sarniensis, the crimson Guernsey Lily, and its hybrids, are the most prolific. Popular, too, is N. curvifolia, especially the variety Fothergellii major, brilliant and beautiful in iridescent scarlet. N. filifolia is evergreen, bright red, with long pistils and stamens. N. Bowdenii, a late summer bloomer, has large pink flowers with rosy lines down the center of each petal. Many named hybrids are also available.

Cool greenhouse: 50°F.

Propagation: By offsets that flower in two to three years. They are best separated after making several years of growth and when the bulb is dormant. Good hybrids are obtained from well-ripened seed sown in flats or bulb pans during February. To get as much growth as possible the first year, transplant as soon as large enough to handle.

Potting: Bulbs 1 to 2 inches in diameter may be planted singly in 4-inch pots, or two or three in a 5- or 6-inch pot, depending on size of bulb. Grow in the same pots for four or five years; plants flower best if roots are undisturbed. Top-dress with fresh soil in August, and take care when removing old soil.

Culture: Nerine wants a loose fibrous soil with peatmoss, leafmold, or sand, added as necessary to keep it light and provide good drainage. Let the soil be fairly dry until growth appears, then soak thoroughly, and continue to water well through the growing cycle. Feed with a complete liquid fertilizer, or manure water every ten days, or with ammonium sulphate or nitrate of soda—1 teaspoon to 1 gallon of water. Grow plants in full sunlight at 45° to 50°, for they will not stand hard forcing. Flowering may be delayed until December and January if plants are kept on the dry side until November. After flowering, it is important to keep plants growing in the sunshine, for it is during this period that they recover strength to flower again the following year. When leaves turn yellow and die back, let the soil dry off completely. Such drying off is necessary to bulbs of this kind.

Pests: Aphids and red spider.

NERIUM (OLEANDER)

Easy Spring-to-Fall Radiance

An old-fashioned ornamental evergreen that makes a grand show from spring to fall. While we usually think of this as a very large plant, it is suited to the home greenhouse since it can be flowered in any size pot from a 7-inch up. Any variety you can find is suitable. Clusters of large yellow, pink, red, or white blooms are borne on vigorous willowy stems. Leaves are narrow and pointed. Both flowers and leaves are poisonous to eat.

Cool greenhouse: 45°F.

Propagation: By cuttings from mature wood that root easily any time in spring, summer, or fall. Stick cuttings in 3-inch pots of peatmoss or loamy soil.

Potting: Transfer directly to 6- or 7-inch pots and shift on up to the size pot or tub desired. In repotting, loosen the ball with your fingers. Then spread out the roots in new soil. Use a potting stick and pot medium hard.

Culture: Oleander is of easy culture, if handled properly. It does well in a medium loamy soil or in peatmoss. The chief requisites to beautiful flowering plants are ample sunlight, proper pruning after flowering, and a rest during winter. Flowering occurs only on mature wood of well-ripened shoots, so plenty of air is needed, especially during fall and winter. Syringe daily during the summer and remove young shoots that appear underneath the flower bud; otherwise, blooms will be hidden by foliage. After plants have flowered, cut them back to encourage a little growth before winter. Very hard pruning is not desirable. Rest during winter in a cool greenhouse at 45° to 50°. Keep on the dry side until spring, but do not let soil get too dry. Water just enough to keep stems fresh or flower buds will drop. In summer, set plants outside in full sunlight.

Pests: Red spider, scale, aphids, and mealy bug.

Oleander (See NERIUM.)

ORNITHOGALUM

Something Different for Winter

A bulb with cup-shaped blooms rather like those of the lily. The fragrant clusters radiate from a single leafless stalk, 2 feet or so high. Colors range from white to yellow. Each bulb produces six to twenty flowers in midwinter, depending on variety. Leaves are long and narrow, usually to about 1 foot. O. arabicum is most commonly grown and one of the showiest. It has large-petaled white flowers with a greenish eye and shiny black pistils. O. lacteum has dense clusters of milk-white flowers about three-quarters of an inch long. O. Saundersiae is similar but a little larger. Pistils are a shiny greenish black. O. thyrsoides is one of the easiest, earlier flowering than arabicum, also white, but with a brown center. There are several hybrids of thyrsoides that are reported good; O. T. aureum (Chincherichee), has golden yellow flowers.

Moderate to warm greenhouse: 55° to 65°F.

Propagation: By offsets removed when repotting. Bulbs multiply readily and reach flowering size the second year.

Potting: Plant 6 or 7 bulbs to a 6- or 8-inch bulb pan. Replant each year between September and December.

Culture: Ornithogalum is of easy culture and does well in any well-drained sandy loam. Keep bulb pans in the cold frame before growth starts, just as you would other bulbs of the lily family. They must not be permitted to freeze, however, and should be brought into the greenhouse before deep freezing weather sets in. Water moderately at all times, especially until growth starts. Staking and tying are necessary for the tall, delicate, flowering stalks. After bloom is over, keep foliage growing and let bulbs dry off gradually. Then store until the following season in the same pots in which they grew.

Pests: Aphids.

OXALIS

Dainty Flowers and Shamrock Foliage

Bulbous or tuberous-rooted plants with long, drooping foliage, ideal for hanging baskets as well as pots. The delicate flowers are white, bright yellow, or pastel shades of pink, red, and violet. Some varieties are practically everblooming; others flower in winter, spring, and summer. I like to set the everblooming variety, rubra, in the rock garden for the summer and then lift some of the best plants for winter flowering in the greenhouse. Some plants survive outdoors with light mulching. Of course, plants that have flowered outdoors all summer will not bloom in the greenhouse in fall until they have rested four to six weeks. A large number of species and hybrids are available. O. Bowieana is rose red. O. cernua, the Bermuda Buttercup, has bright yellow flowers from February on; O. hirta has large rose-pink flowers and feathery foliage; O. lasiandra is carmine. O. rubra (illustrated) and crassipes are the best everblooming types with deep-veined rose flowers.

Cool to warm greenhouse: 45° to 60°F.

Propagation: By division of tubers or from offsets that increase rapidly. Early kinds are divided and planted in August or September. Everblooming varieties may be separated at any time, but plants are set back less if divided in January or

February. Seed germinates rapidly in February and March. Grow in light soil at 60°. Some varieties form seeds readily and even become a weed in walks and under benches.

Potting: Line an 8-inch wire basket with an inch of sphagnum moss and fill with soil. Push 4 to 6 tubers into the soil about half an inch deep. For pot culture, plant three or four tubers to a 5-inch pan, or singly in 3- or 4-inch pots. Replant in fresh soil each season.

Culture: Oxalis likes an acid soil and does well in a mixture of one-half peatmoss or leafmold mixed with light compost and sand. The soil in which dormant tubers are started should be kept fairly moist but not watered heavily until growth starts. Feed with a solution of ammonium sulphate—1 teaspoon to 1 gallon of water—or with a complete liquid fertilizer to encourage the production of good flowers. Oxalis must have full sun to produce abundantly. Blooms close at night and also on dull days. Beyond the removal of dead foliage now and then, this plant requires little attention, though the tubers of some varieties are likely to push up out of the soil after a time. These may be set deeper when plants are repotted. Summer- and fall-flowering varieties require a rest in winter. Store tubers in the pots in which they grew, or in paper bags with dry sand or peatmoss.

Pests: Green fly.

PAROCHETUS COMMUNIS — SHAMROCK-PEA or BLUE OXALIS

A Pink-and-Blue Everblooming Creeper

A trailing relative of sweet clover with pea-shaped flowers of brilliant blue with pink wings. The foliage is like that of oxalis and marked with a brown crescent. The plant is excellent either for pots or hanging baskets since it blooms nearly all year. It is useful for softening the edge of the greenhouse bench.

Cool greenhouse: 45° to 50°F.

Propagation: By cuttings that root practically any time; by division of roots when repotting is done in February or March; by seed. For the healthiest and best-looking plants, start new ones every other year.

Potting: Transfer small plants to 3-inch pots, then on to 6- or 8-inch baskets. For a quick show, set three or four plants in one container. For edging along greenhouse benches, set plants about 8 inches apart.

Culture: Grow in a loose fibrous soil, and feed once a week when plants are well established. Shade from March to September. Water moderately during summer, but keep on the dry side the rest of the year. Plants may be set out in the rock garden in summer and lifted again in fall.

Pests: Aphids, thrips, and mealy bug.

PASITHEA CAERULEA

Sprays of February Blue

A bulbous plant of the lily family from Chile. The loose clusters of blue flowers are an inch and a half across and appear above grassy foliage in late winter or early spring. They last at least a week and are most welcome, since they come at a time when there is little blue in the greenhouse.

Cool greenhouse: 50°F.

Culture: Treat the same as Ornithogalum (which see).

PASSIFLORA PASSION FLOWER

Odd Flowers to Steal the Show

A climbing vine with large, charming flowers of intricate formation. P. alato-caerulea (Pfordtii) one of the loveliest and easiest to grow, bears fragrant flowers up to 4 inches in white and shades of pink with a crown of purple, blue, and white, all within the same bloom. The plant is vigorous but easily controlled in the medium-to-large greenhouse or lean-to. Depending on temperature, it can be brought into bloom in March or later.

Moderate to warm greenhouse: 55° to 65°F.

Propagation: By 3- to 4-inch cuttings of half-ripened wood. They can be stuck right in pots of peatmoss and sand. Take two or three cuttings, and later select the strongest, for only one plant will be wanted to a pot.

Potting: Transfer the best rooted cutting to a 5-inch pot; then shift on up to a 10 or 12, if plant is to be grown in a pot. It will do better in a ground bed having 8 to 10 inches of soil.

Culture: Passiflora is not too particular as to soil so long as good drainage is provided. It requires little attention other than feeding every two weeks with liquid fertilizer while in active growth; syringing every day or two in bright weather; and pruning, after flowers are gone, or just before new growth starts in January. If young tender shoots are cut out as they appear, the others will grow stronger. Shade lightly in summer, and never let plants suffer for lack of water. Passiflora can be grown at 55° during the winter, but will take forcing and bloom earlier at 65°. The plant will do well for several years in the same pot or bed if the exhausted top soil is replaced with fresh each January.

Pests: Mealy bug, scale, and red spider.

Passion Flower (See PASSIFLORA.)

PENTAS LANCEOLATA

Lilac, White, or Crimson for Winter

A compact winter-flowering shrub up to 2 feet resembling Bouvardia and of the same family. It bears twenty or more tubular flowers in a flat 3-inch cluster. The species, P. lanceolata, has lilac blossoms, but its varieties, coccinea in deep crimson, and alba in creamy white, are of better form and color.

Warm greenhouse: 60° to 65°F.

Propagation: By cuttings of half-mature wood taken in March or April. They root readily at 70°.

Potting: Transfer to 3-inch pots before roots get too long. Place in the shade until plants take hold, and then give full sun. Before the root ball becomes pot bound, move to 5-inch pots. Repot in 8-inch pots the following spring after flowering.

Culture: A fibrous loam lightened with decayed manure or leafmold is good. Pinch two or three times during the summer, and feed with liquid manure or a complete fertilizer after roots have become well established. Give all sun available from fall to spring, but shade and give plenty of fresh air from April to September. Water moderately from spring through fall. Keep on the dry side during winter, but never permit soil to get so dry that foliage wilts. To induce branching pinch back new growth as soon as it starts in spring. Old plants may be grown on for several years, but new ones started every other year from cuttings flower much more profusely.

Pests: Scale and mealy bug.

PHLOGACANTHUS FLAME FLOWER

Orange-flowering Ornamental

An herbaceous shrub that flowers freely in spring or early summer under light airy conditions. The variety thyrsiflorus, a handsome plant with flaming orange flowers in dense terminal spikes, is the only one grown.

Warm greenhouse: 65°F.

Propagation: By seed, which is always available but slow to germinate, or by cuttings taken in early spring. These root readily at a temperature of 65° to 70°.

Potting: Transplant to 3-inch pots and transfer to 6's or 8's in about two months. Repot in fresh soil after flowering, scraping off old soil from the surface and sides of the root ball. A 10-inch pot may be necessary.

Culture: Plant in light fibrous loam with one-third peatmoss and coarse sand added to provide good drainage. Pinch young plants to encourage side shoots, and pinch two or three times to keep plants in good form. Maintain high humidity and water liberally while the plant is making growth, especially when pots become filled with roots. Feed with liquid fertilizer every three to four weeks. Shade during summer, and syringe during bright weather.

Pests: Aphids and red spider.

PIMELEA RICE FLOWER

April Shower of Bloom

An Australian evergreen similar to heather. It is free-flowering, and the plant is literally covered with minute white, pink, or reddish flowers in early spring. Garden books list and describe a number of species, but I have only been able to get one, P. coarctica, a neat dwarf with abundant white flowers and white fruit. Perhaps this scarcity is due to a falling off in popularity of the plant during the past twenty-five years, for I have never come across it in an amateur greenhouse.

Cool greenhouse: 45° to 50°F.

Propagation: In March, 3- to 4-inch cuttings of half-ripened wood, grown at 55° to 60°. These should make small flowering plants in a year.

Potting: Transfer rooted cuttings to 3- or 4-inch pots. By fall, the slow-growing plants should be ready for 5's or 6's. Transfer to slightly larger pots each year.

Culture: Pimeleas like a light soil of loam, peatmoss, and sand in equal parts. Keep moderately moist at all times. Pinch as soon as a little growth is made, and continue to pinch to keep plants in good form. They will flower when quite young, but it is advisable to pick off the first blooms to let strength go to the roots. Dense shade and daily syringing are important during the summer. Feed with liquid fertilizer every ten days to 2 weeks.

Pests: Red spider.

Pineapple Lily (See EUCOMIS.)
Pleroma (See TIBOUCHINA.)

PLUMBAGO LEADWORT

Semi-Climber with Blue "Phlox" Flowers

The ease with which this drooping semi-climber can be controlled makes it ideal for the small greenhouse. It flowers well as a 6-inch pot plant and may be grown as such for years. Blooms that resemble phlox appear in loose clusters on tips of new growth, last for several weeks, and continue in succession through late spring and summer. The flowers of P. capensis vary from azure blue to white, and there is its white variety, alba. Both are handsome, starting to flower when 2 to 4 feet high. They are rarely without bloom. P. indica (rosea) coccinea, with maroon flowers is most satisfactory for early forcing in 6-inch pots.

Cool greenhouse: 45° to 50°F.

Propagation: By 4- to 5-inch cuttings of half-ripened wood taken in spring or fall. Root these in a 3-inch pot at 60°. P. capensis grows readily from seed that is usually available. P. indica does not usually do well from seed.

Potting: Rooted cuttings in 3-inch pots will be ready for 6's in about two months. Continue to shift to pots of larger size if bigger plants are wanted. Repot small plants after flowering, scraping off about one-third of the old soil from the root balls and replanting in pots of the same size or larger. Top-dress large plants by removing a few inches of old soil from the surface and replacing it with fresh. When planted in a well drained ground bed, plants can be grown so as to cover completely the back wall of a greenhouse.

Culture: This is a strong-rooted plant and does well in a fairly fibrous, decayed sod loam with about one-fifth sand added. It wants high humidity and shade during spring and summer. Grow in full sun the rest of the year. Give young plants plenty of sun and pinch back all straggling growth to about 8 inches. With good handling, plants have been kept flowering intermittently most of the year. A cool temperature of 40° is best in early winter. In February, if this is increased to 50°, new growth will start immediately, since Plumbago responds well to forcing. Feed twice a week with complete liquid fertilizer to get strong root growth and large flower heads. A wire or trellis is needed for large plants. After flowering is over, cut back shoots to about 12 inches. This will produce good new growth for the next season's bloom.

Pests: Mealy bug.

POINCIANA (CAESALPINIA)

Orange and Yellow on a Tropical Shrub

A spring- and summer-flowering shrub with bright showy panicles and feathery foliage. Although it grows 10 to 12 feet tall in the South, it flowers in a 6-inch pot under glass. P. pulcherrima (Caesalpinia poinciana), Barbados Pride, has yellow-orange flowers with long, bright red stamens and somewhat prickly stems, variety flava (illustrated) and P. Gilliesii (Caesalpinia Gilliesii) are both yellow.

Warm greenhouse: 60° to 65°F. and humid conditions for P. pulcherrima and its varieties.

Cool greenhouse: 50°F. for P. Gilliesii.

Propagation: By seed, soaked in warm water for several hours, and sown in sandy soil. Shade until growth is well established. Cuttings are difficult to root, but sometimes take in a closed case at 75° if selected when the parent plant is in vigorous growth.

Potting: Transfer seedlings to small pots of loose but poor soil as soon as true leaves appear. Growth is rapid and plants will be ready for 6-inch pots within eight weeks. Shift to larger pots each fall, as required. Top-dress old plants each year with fresh soil.

Culture: Use rich porous soil for second and succeeding pottings. Water freely while growth is active but moderately during short days from December through February. Shade from spring to fall, but give full sun in winter.

Pests: Aphids, scale, and mealy bug.

POLYGALA DALMAISIANA

"Sweet Peas" on an Evergreen

An evergreen, 2 to 3 feet high, with showy clusters of magenta flowers and neat, light green foliage. It blooms on ripened wood intermittently through the year, but is at its best during February and March.

Cool greenhouse: 45° to 50°F.

Propagation: By cuttings in spring that root at a temperature of 50°.

Potting: Transfer rooted cuttings to 3-inch pots, and keep in a moist shaded location. Repot in 5- or 6-inch pots as soon as roots are well developed. Repot each spring.

Culture: Polygala wants a loose, well-drained soil lightened with peatmoss or rotted manure. Water freely during summer but moderately other times. Syringe twice daily in bright weather, except when in bloom. Feed young plants two or three times until they are well established. Plants may be plunged out-of-doors from June to September in a shaded place.

Pests: Scale.

RAPHIOLEPIS INDICA INDIA-HAWTHORN

Blush Stars On a Dwarf Shrub

An evergreen with small star-shaped pinkish white flowers in loose panicles from April to early May. The foliage is attractive with rounded, shiny, dark green leaves. Although this plant reaches 2 to 3 feet, it is a slow grower and never requires more than a 6- or 8-inch pot under glass—then, only after four or five years.

Cool greenhouse: 45° to 50°F.

Propagation: By cuttings of ripened wood in spring or summer, or seed sown in spring. One or two of these plants will probably be sufficient in a small greenhouse.

Potting: Transfer cuttings to 3- or 4-inch pots, depending on size of roots. In a few months they should be ready for 5's or 6's. Repot in the same sized pot the following year, or top-dress with fresh soil.

Culture: This plant is easily grown in a mixture of loam and peatmoss with a little sand. Feed with a complete fertilizer or manure water every two weeks during the summer to get growth well established. Syringe daily in bright weather and shade partially from hot summer sun.

Pests: Aphids, thrips, red spider, mealy bug, and scale.

Redhot Cat-Tail (See ACALYPHA.)

REINWARDTIA INDICA YELLOW FLAX

Golden "Flax" for the Small Greenhouse

A splendid spring-flowering plant of shrubby twining growth. It never reaches more than 2 to 3 feet and produces three or four bright, flaxlike yellow flowers, 1 to 2 inches across in terminal clusters.

Moderate to warm greenhouse: 55° to 60°F.

Propagation: By basal cuttings of strong growth, when available, rooted at 60° to 65°. (Top growth will root but rarely makes good plants.) Plants set out for the summer usually provide good cutting stock in fall. Root directly in 3-inch pots of peatmoss and sand or sandy loam, since young plants do not transplant well. Pinch off the ends of shoots when 3 inches long and again when an additional 3 inches of growth is made.

Potting: Transfer young plants to 6-inch pots in late spring. If they are grown for more than one year, repot in 8's, or topdress in fall just after growth starts.

Culture: Grow in a light soil of fibrous loam and peatmoss. Shade lightly from spring until September, but grow in full sun the rest of the year. Syringe daily in summer and provide dense humidity. Continue to pinch two or three times to give compact form, and remove all flower buds until plants are well established in 6-inch pots. Reinwardtia may be set outdoors in partial shade for the summer, cut back, and brought into the greenhouse about the end of August. Old plants may be grown on for two or three years, but new ones raised from cuttings every other year are more satisfactory.

Pests: Red spider and aphids.

Rhynchospermum (See TRACHELOSPERMUM.)
Rice Flower (See PIMELEA.)

RIVINA HUMILIS ROUGE PLANT

Decorative Red Berries for Variety

Try this plant if you would like something with ornamental berries for color and variety. The flowers are insignificant, small and pinkish white, but the long drooping clusters of brilliant red berries that follow in late spring and summer are most decorative. The plant I grew flowered and produced berries in a 5-inch pot before it was 2 feet high.

Warm greenhouse: 65°F.

Propagation: By seed sown in March. It germinates well at 60°. Plants often self-sow in the gravel or sand of a bench, so you have a succession of new ones coming along naturally each year. Cuttings taken of half-mature wood root readily any time they are available.

Potting: Transfer young plants to 3-inch pots, and then on to 5's or 6's before they become pot bound.

Culture: Rivina practically takes care of itself. Grow in any good loam, and pinch two or three times to induce branching. Feed every ten days with a solution of ammonium sulphate or nitrate of soda—1 teaspoon to 1 gallon of water. This plant can stand plenty of feeding and water when making growth.

Syringe daily during bright weather until blossoms appear. Then discontinue feeding and keep moderately moist.

Pests: Red spider and mealy bug.

ROCHEA COCCINEA

Scarlet Show for Summer

A shrubby succulent pleasing for its large, fragrant, scarlet clusters. Among the showiest of greenhouse plants, it grows 1 to 2 feet high.

Cool greenhouse: 45°F.

Propagation: By about 4-inch cuttings taken in March. These root readily at 50° in sand or peatmoss. Take care not to keep the medium too wet or ends will rot. Rooting occurs within a few weeks. Plants are also easily raised to flowering size from seed in about 18 months.

Potting: Set young plants in 3-inch pots. After an inch or so of growth is made, pinch and shift to 5's. Repot in fresh soil and, after flowering, shift to pots one or two sizes larger.

Culture: As with other succulents, use a well-drained sandy soil so roots will not rot. Soggy conditions are ruinous. During summer, plants may be plunged in the garden in full sunshine, if shelter is provided from heavy rains. Feed with a complete liquid fertilizer every two weeks. This is important, especially after pots are filled with roots. Plants can be flowered the second summer if they are cut back to 6 inches and pinched, after new growth starts, to induce branching.

Pests: Aphids.

ROELLA CILIATA

Saucy Blue Bells in Spring

A shrubby plant with upright flowers of unusual markings. Each light blue bell is circled with a black ring, which in turn, is circled with white. Foliage is small, and plants are so covered with blooms in spring that leaves are completely hidden.

Cool greenhouse: 45° to 50°F.

Propagation: By cuttings that root readily in April in a mixture of sand and sphagnum moss, or in vermiculite. Seed is available but difficult to germinate.

Potting: Plant cuttings in 3-inch pots and pinch as soon as growth starts. Spring cuttings should be ready for 6-inch pots by midsummer. Transfer to 8's the following spring.

Culture: Grow in loose fibrous soil that drains freely. Add peatmoss and sand if soil is clayey. Roella flowers when quite small, but first blooms should be removed to produce good flowering specimens. Shade from bright sun during spring and summer. These plants are subject to mildew so avoid drafts, sudden changes in temperature, and condensation on foliage. Remove dead foliage at all times.

Pests: Brown scale.

Rogiera (See RONDELETIA.)

RONDELETIA (ROGIERA)

Evergreen and Everblooming

An evergreen shrub, almost always in bloom. Although this plant eventually reaches 4 to 5 feet, it blooms before it grows to 2 feet. Flower clusters resemble those of lantana. R. amoena, and R. cordata (illustrated) are bright pink with yellow throats. R. odorata, sometimes seen but apparently not listed in catalogs, is coral-red with an orange-yellow throat.

Moderate to warm greenhouse: 55° to 60°F.

Propagation: By cuttings of half-ripened shoots. These root in about four weeks at 70° at any time of year but best in spring. Use a mixture of sand and peatmoss, or vermiculite. Growth is slow so it is better to buy established plants.

Potting: Pot quite firmly in 3's immediately after rooting. Spring cuttings should be ready for 5's or 6's in July. Transfer to larger pots the following July, if larger plants are wanted. Condition and size of roots will indicate the size pot for each shift. If properly fed, plants that have reached 8's can go for two seasons without repotting.

Culture: Grow in a mixture of one part loam and two parts peatmoss with a little sand added to insure drainage. A humid atmosphere is necessary, especially during early growth. Pinch young shoots several times, for this plant is difficult to shape after growth is hardened. Full sun is essential to healthy growth, and only light shade is needed during the hottest part of the summer. Syringe daily from spring until fall, and on bright days during the winter. While the plant is growing, feed with liquid manure or a complete liquid fertilizer once a week. During the winter, keep only moderately moist, and discontinue feeding. Remove dead flowers but don't take much stem.

Pests: Mealy bug, scale, and thrips.

Rouge Plant (See RIVINA.)

RUSSELIA EQUISETIFORMIS CORAL PLANT

Green and Coral for a Basket

A rushlike shrub of beautiful habit with drooping, light green branches in pleasant contrast to long sprays of tubular coral flowers. It is excellent for pots or baskets since blooms are almost continuous, and under glass, plants do not grow over 3 to 4 feet high.

Moderate to warm greenhouse: 55° to 60°F.

Propagation: By cuttings in spring that root in three to four weeks. Set directly in a 3-inch pot filled with sand or peatmoss. Plunge in cinders or sand to provide even moisture.

Potting: Transfer to 5- or 6-inch pots, then on to 7's or 8's, when the first ones are filled with roots, or plant singly in 6- or 8-inch baskets lined with sphagnum moss. Repot each spring.

Culture: Use fibrous soil and grow in partial shade. Syringe daily in summer, and water freely except during dull days from December to March. To keep plants in good form, prune lightly during February.

Pests: Mealy bug and scale.

Saxifraga (See BERGENIA.)
Scarborough Lily (See VALLOTA.)

SCHIZOSTYLIS COCCINEA — KAFIR LILY

Pink or Red Lilies for Fall

A member of the iris family with sprays of ten to fourteen brilliant scarlet flowers on 1- to 2-foot spikes. Blooms are excellent for cutting from October to late December, when flowers of this type are especially desirable. A hybrid, Mrs. Hegarty, is available with deep pink flowers.

Cool greenhouse: 50°F.

Propagation: By division of roots in spring. Take each with three to five buds. Plant out in the garden about 8 inches apart, and lift toward the end of August. Plant in 6-inch or smaller pots depending on the size and condition of roots. Seed can be germinated but will take two or three years to produce flowering plants. Buy dormant rhizomes which are available from suppliers in the early spring.

Potting: Grow as a pot plant, or for cut flowers, in deep seed flats. Plant in 6-inch pots or set rhizomes 6 inches apart in flats.

Culture: Pot in loose, fibrous, decayed sod loam in the fall. After growth starts, keep well watered. Feed with a complete liquid fertilizer right through the blooming period, and until foliage is fully matured. When this dies back after flowering, store plants dry in pots in which they grew. Put them under a bench, if they will not be damaged by dripping water, or in a protected cold frame until spring. Then they may be set out in the garden again and handled the same as the previous year.

Pests: Thrips.

Sea Daffodil (See ISMENE.)

SEDUM

Handsome Decoration for Shelves

Among tender succulent sedums are several that flower beautifully in baskets. They are also useful as pot plants for shelves where foliage and flowers can droop gracefully along the eave line. Few plants are easier to cultivate or more desirable for the purpose. S. Sieboldii (illustrated) bears branched clusters of fine pink flowers in fall. S. Palmeri, a deep orange with spreading, drooping branches, flowers in early spring. S. mexicanum is summer blooming with yellow flowers.

Cool to moderate greenhouse: 50° to 55°F.

Propagation: By cuttings, seed, or division. Cuttings of leafy stems are taken in spring and rooted in sand or vermiculite. Take care not to keep the medium so wet that ends rot. Plants bloom the first year, but will not be at their best until the second. Each leaf can be rooted in sand, but this is hardly worthwhile if cuttings are available. Seed is sown in spring, but plants usually take two to three years to reach flowering size.

Potting: Plant divisions in 6- to 8-inch pans or baskets depending on size of roots. For a quick show, rooted cuttings can be set five or six to a container. They can also be planted in 3-inch pots and shifted the second year to 5- or 6-inch pans. Tall growers will need 6- to 8-inch pans.

Culture: Sedums need free drainage, a coarse porous soil, and lots of sun. Water cautiously at first, and rather moderately after roots have filled the pot. Overwatering must be avoided, but do not permit soil to get dry, except when plants rest after flowering.

Pests: Sucking insects.

SENECIO PETASITIS CALIFORNIA GERANIUM

Profusion of Yellow Daisies

A Mexican shrub that makes a bold show with immense terminal trusses of bright yellow daisies appearing in February and continuing until early spring. Stems are sturdy and extend well above large, felty leaves. Although this is a large, tropical plant, it flowers in small pots when but 2 feet high. The nice thing about it is that it can easily be controlled to 3 or 4 feet in large pots or small tubs.

Cool greenhouse: 50°F.

Propagation: By cuttings in June or July. These will reach flowering size the following winter.

Potting: Transfer rooted cuttings to 4-inch pots in August. These should be ready for 6's by late fall. Transfer to 8's or

9's the second year. Repot every June thereafter in the same-sized pot or one a size smaller, shaking old soil from roots.

Culture: Plant in loose, rich, heavy soil. Feed with a weak solution of liquid fertilizer every two weeks after plants become well established. No pinching is necessary, since this is a naturally compact grower. Prune after flowering and rest by keeping soil moderately moist until June.

Pests: Red spider, green fly, and thrips.

Senna (See CASSIA.)
Shamrock-Pea (See PAROCHETUS.)

SINNINGIA SPECIOSA GLOXINIA

Jewel Colors and Velvet Texture

A summer-flowering plant with flowers of rare beauty. The soft bell-shaped blooms come in rich blue, violet, purple, rose, red, or white. Many are spotted or marbled with dark tones against light backgrounds. Blooms rise 6 inches above large, downy leaves.

Warm greenhouse: 60°F.

Propagation: Generally from tubers planted in February or March, also from seeds and leaf cuttings. Tubers are spread out in a flat of peatmoss at 65° to 70°. Keep on dry side at first but water well after growth starts. The earliest to root will flower in June. All tubers will not start at once, so a succession of blooms is possible until late fall, if enough tubers are started. Stronger plants that produce more blooms are grown from seed rather than tubers. Sowings are made during December and January for blooms by July. Seedlings are set 3 or 4 inches apart in a second flat and grown until they become 4 to 6 inches high. Vermiculite or a mixture of peatmoss and loam, with sand added, make good mediums.

To multiply a stock of rare varieties, leaf cuttings are best. Plants form on the cut ends of leaf stems stuck in moist peatmoss. Some gardeners succeed in handling leaf cuttings in the same manner as for rex begonias, but mine always rot. The midrib of the leaf is cut across four or five places and secured in sand with pebbles. Roots form at the cuts and produce new small plants.

Potting: Transfer young plants to 4- or 5-inch pots. Then shift to 6's. Replant tubers in fresh soil each year.

Culture: Most gardeners grow gloxinias in a loose potting mixture of soil and peatmoss, but I prefer peatmoss with a little sphagnum moss. In either mixture, keep roots very moist. Sub-irrigation is excellent for this plant because water must be kept off the foliage. Protection from sun is necessary from spring to fall, but plants will not burn readily if they are well supplied with moisture. After flowering is over and leaves turn yellow, store tubers in the pots of soil in which they grew. Set them under a bench, provided temperature will not fall below 45° and water will not drip on them. Soil should be kept dry during this period except for a possible very light syringing around the pots to keep tubers from shriveling. Where space is limited, tubers may be removed from old soil after flowering, and stored in paper bags with dry sand or peatmoss to keep air from them.

Pests: Mite, possibly mealy bug, and mildew.

Smithiantha (See NAEGELIA.)

SOLANUM JASMINOIDES

White Stars On a Slender Climber

A delicate woody climber with eight to twelve star-shaped, fragrant, white flowers in dense clusters nearly three inches long. It can be well recommended for any size greenhouse because it starts to flower when very young and is almost continuously in bloom from then on. You need not fear that it is one of those climbers that will take over the greenhouse either, because even mature plants can be controlled within 3 to 4 feet. The one I have is proof of the plants half-hardiness too, for it arrived by express during mid-winter with the soil partly frozen. After a little coddling, it gradually overcame the set back and from then on has been doing nobly.

Cool greenhouse: 50°F.

Propagation: By cuttings of young shoots taken in early spring. These produce flowering plants by fall.

Potting: Transfer rooted cuttings to 3-inch pots. Move to 4's or 5's when ready. Repot or top-dress each spring.

Culture: Grow in loam, leafmold, and sand. Water freely in spring and summer but moderately the rest of the year. Feed with weak liquid manure or fertilizer two or three times in spring. Pinch straggling shoots to develop good form. Train on bamboo stakes or a light wire trellis. Syringe during hot weather, and shade lightly.

Pests: Aphids and scale.

Sparaxis (See IRIS FAMILY.)

SPARMANNIA AFRICANA AFRICAN HEMP

Heavy Heads of White in Winter

An evergreen winter-flowering shrub with clusters of unusual white, yellow-stamened flowers that remind you of the snowballs of viburnum, but are much more attractive and very long lasting. The plant makes a small symmetrical tree, particularly well suited to the medium-sized or larger greenhouse, and its foliage in compact masses of broad leaves is always good looking. Specimens are at their best when 3 to 4 feet tall, but plants begin to flower when small.

Cool to moderate greenhouse: 50° to 55°F.

Propagation: By cuttings that root readily in early spring at 70°.

Potting: When they are well rooted, transfer cuttings to 3-inch pots. In five to six weeks, they will be ready for 6's, and two months later, for 8's or 10's. Repot in fresh soil during March or April.

Culture: This hemp is not particular as to soil but good drainage is essential. Pinch tips of young shoots two or three times. Water well during the spring- and summer-growing season, and syringe daily. Give all sunlight possible in winter, but grow in partial shade during bright hot weather. Plants may be plunged outdoors in a semi-shaded location if desired. Feed when young with a complete liquid fertilizer every ten days. Prune into shape and keep on the dry side after flowering. Mature plants may be grown on for several years, but it is better to root new ones from cuttings every other year.

Pests: Red spider, aphids, and practically all greenhouse insects.

SPATHIPHYLLUM

Long-lasting Green-to-White Spathes

A plant much like Anthurium but smaller and more delicate. It is in "flower" from early spring through May. The inflorescence (not a true flower), lasts for months under glass and is freely borne. First it is white and then green. S. floribundum, the best dwarf variety, is usually grown, though S. Clevelandii is also listed.

Warm greenhouse: 65° to 70°F.

Propagation: By division when plants are resting.

Potting: Plant in 4-inch pots when small, then in 6's or larger pots, depending on size of root stock.

Culture: Grow in equal parts leafmold and peatmoss with a little loam and sharp sand added. During the growing season, keep soil moist but never saturated. Syringe daily and feed with liquid manure from spring on, to get healthy plants with abundant blooms. Rest, by withholding water, during the dull days of winter, but do not allow soil to get so dry that leaves wilt. Heat is essential to good development, 65° to 70°. Orchid-house conditions suit Spathiphyllum very well.

Pests: Aphids, thrips, mealy bug, and scale.

Spider Lily (See ISMENE.)
Spring Star Flower (See BRODIAEA.)
Star Jasmine (See TRACHELOSPERMUM.)

STEPHANOTIS FLORIBUNDA MADAGASCAR JASMINE

Fragrance from Spring to Fall

An excellent climber for the medium-sized or large greenhouse. The pure white, starry blooms are produced in clusters and open in charming succession from spring to fall. Sweet fragrance and lasting quality make this "jasmine" fine for corsages. When not in flower, the plant is also attractive with its firm, glossy leaves. Grow this one on a trellis or twine it up the north side of the house.

Warm greenhouse: 60° to 65°F.

Propagation: By cuttings—three or four joints from half-ripened wood—that root easily in a closed case any time of year at 70°. The best plants are started in spring and rooted in a mixture of sand and peatmoss. They reach flowering size in a year. You will probably want only one of such a sturdy climber, so start only two or three shoots and select the strongest.

Potting: Transfer the chosen cutting to a 3- or 4-inch pot and set firmly. Watch out that it doesn't get root-bound. Shift as needed to a pot 2 or 3 inches larger, and pinch when 18 inches high. From here on, it may be grown for 10-, 12-inch, or even larger pots or tubs, but Stephanotis is at its best set in a ground bed. It will thrive in the same pot or bed for several years if annually top-dressed with fresh soil.

Culture: Stephanotis forms flower buds at 60° and it is useless to grow it cooler. In fact, 65° is best. A good fibrous soil with sand added for drainage is essential, and a heavy mulch of peatmoss or manure is beneficial from early spring to fall to hold in moisture. Syringe daily and provide a dense shade during warm weather until September. Feed with a complete liquid fertilizer every two weeks from spring until fall. After flowering is over, trim plants back to keep them in good form.

Pests: Mealy bug and scale.

STRELITZIA REGINAE — BIRD-OF-PARADISE FLOWER

Flaming Forms of Orange and Blue

A South African plant, magnificent for foliage as well as its blooms of bright orange and blue which resemble a bird poised for flight. Each inflorescence consists of about 6 flowers that develop from a long, almost horizontal, purplish bract. The plants are large, 3 to 4 feet tall, but I have had two excellent specimens flowering in 7-inch pots. Early spring or summer flowers last well and are popular for arrangements and corsages.

Warm greenhouse: 60° to 65°F.

Propagation: By suckers or division. Since only well-established plants will flower, it is advisable to buy large-sized plants. Division of old plants and potting of suckers is done in spring when weather is mild and humid. Pot firmly and give plenty of heat, 65° to 70°, to get into growth; otherwise roots may rot.

Potting: Strelitzias require 8-to-10-inch pots depending on size. Ram the soil firmly around the root ball. Plants may be grown on in the same pot for several years. When repotting is necessary, do it in early spring.

Culture: Plants need good drainage and a rich sandy loam. Add coarse sand and peatmoss up to a third by volume, if your soil is clayey. Grow in full sun through the winter, but provide a light shade during hot summer weather. Keep on the dry side during the dead of winter, when the plant is resting, but supply plenty of moisture as growth starts. Then feed once a week with ammonium sulphate—1 teaspoon to a gallon of water—or with manure water. This plant will stand plenty of rough treatment but will not flower unless in good health and with ten or more leaves.

Pests: Aphids, scale, and mealy bug.

Streptanthera (See IRIS FAMILY.)

STREPTOCARPUS CAPE PRIMROSE

Velvet Bells from Spring to Fall

A showy plant with beautiful bright blue or purple flowers, similar to the gloxinia, and broad basal leaves. The striking species, S. Wendlandii, produces violet-blue flowers in clusters on short stems. They rise from the midrib of a large leaf that rests on the soil. Many beautiful low-growing hybrids are available. Plants bloom over a long period in spring, summer or late fall.

Cool to moderate greenhouse: 50° to 55°F.

Propagation: By seed sown from November to January. Seeds are fine and should only be pressed into the surface of the soil. (Some gardeners also report success with leaf cuttings of divisions.)

Potting: Transplant seedlings 2 inches apart in pans or flats. As soon as leaves begin to touch, transfer to 4-inch pots.

Culture: Grow in a light potting mixture of loam, peatmoss or leafmold, and sand. Moisture and shading are essential from spring to fall. When flower stems appear, apply a weak solution of manure water or a complete liquid fertilizer every two to three weeks.

Pests: Aphids.

STROBILANTHES ISOPHYLLUS

A Lavender Shrub from India

A free-blooming, evergreen with narrow, dark green leaves, suggesting the willow. Out of the axil of each leaf, lavender flowers appear in clusters. They open wide all at once from late winter to early spring. The plant never goes beyond 2 to 3 feet under glass, and starts flowering at about 14 inches.

Warm greenhouse: 60° to 65°F.

Propagation: By cuttings of half-mature wood in spring at 80°. Only young plants are attractive, so new stock should be started each year.

Potting: Plant rooted cuttings directly in 4-inch pots. Repot when necessary, depending on the condition of roots, but never to more than a 6-inch pot.

Culture: Provide fibrous loam composted with sod or manure. Add sand if soil is clayey, for good drainage is essential. High humidity and warm-house conditions are needed. Do not attempt to grow under 60°, or foliage will drop. Syringe frequently from spring to fall and cut shoots well back in January.

Pests: Mealy bug, thrips, scale, and aphids.

SUTHERLANDIA FRUTESCENS

Scarlet Clusters from Spring to Summer

A tender branching shrub that grows to 3 feet with showy scarlet flowers about 1 inch long. They appear in clusters on stems that grow out of leaf and branch joints. The foliage is attractive, too, with numerous small gray leaflets.

Cool to moderate greenhouse: 45° to 55°F.

Propagation: By cuttings or seed in March or April.

Culture: Treat the same as Swainsona (which see).

SWAINSONA

Sprays of Red "Sweet Peas"

An herbaceous Australian shrub of free-blooming habit. It grows 2 to 3 feet high and, from late spring into summer produces long-stemmed clusters of flowers that look like sweet peas. S. galegifolia (illustrated) has supple branches and large, dark red flowers, S. Greyana is similar, with pink flowers in more erect racemes. There is also a violet-flowered variety, S. coronillaefolia, that I am told is well worth seeking out, but so far I have not been able to find either seed or plant of it.

Cool to moderate greenhouse: 45° to 55°F.

Propagation: By cuttings or seed in March or April. Seed will germinate more readily if first soaked in water and then sown thinly in sandy soil or vermiculite at 75°.

Potting: Transfer young plants to 3- or 4-inch pots, depending on amount of root growth. By spring, Swainsona should be ready for 6's. If old plants are to be grown on, shift to pots one or two sizes larger each February.

Culture: Use a loose fibrous loam that has been composted with manure, soil that will keep in good condition for a long time. Pinch young shoots when they get to 2 inches. Plunge pots in moist cinders or sand. Syringe daily, and give young plants plenty of shade. Pinch again in July and give more sun, but continue syringing, and water freely until September. Then, keep soil just slightly moist. Train plants on bamboo stakes and prune well after flowering. Old plants that are to be grown on to large specimens require feeding every two weeks during the growing season. Use a complete fertilizer or ammonium sulphate—1 teaspoon to 1 gallon of water.

Pests: Aphids, red spider, and scale.

Synnotia (See IRIS FAMILY.)

TABERNAEMONTANA

Spring Fragrance from Double "Oleanders"

A semi-climbing evergreen with wonderfully fragrant flowers in spring. T. coronaria has white semi-double blooms that look like double oleanders. Those of T. citrifolia are also white, but smaller. T. grandiflora is yellow. Any of the varieties make good pot plants since they flower when 2 to 3 feet high and are easily trained to good form.

Warm greenhouse: 60° to 65°F.

Propagation: By cuttings 4 to 5 inches long of young shoots in spring. These root in a few weeks at 70°.

Potting: Transfer young plants to 3-inch pots and grow in dense humidity to get them started. Move to 6-inch pots after a month or so. The following spring, after flowering, shift to pots one or two sizes larger. Take care not to disturb roots. Top-dress with fresh soil each year.

Culture: Plant in rich sandy soil and keep moderately moist at all times. Syringe daily through spring and summer, except when plants are in flower. Shade during July and August, but grow in full sun the rest of the year. During the summer, feed twice a week with weak manure water or liquid fertilizer. Train the vines around bamboo stakes, a light wire loop, or on a trellis. Prune into shape when flowering is past.

Pests: Mealy bug and scale.

TALINUM FAME FLOWER

Pink, or Red and Yellow Cups

A semi-succulent plant that grows to 18 inches with fleshy ornamental leaves and clusters of small flowers on long stems. It blooms freely in spring and summer on branching stalks. T. calycinum is an 8-inch plant with vivid pink flowers an inch across, larger than those of T. parviflorum which also grows to 8 inches. T. paniculatum, a 2-foot shrub, has reddish-yellow flowers in clusters up to 10 inches long. T. okanoganense is a low-growing species with a profusion of white flowers that are short-lived, but produced in succession. Several other species are available.

Warm greenhouse: 60°F.

Culture: Treat the same as Kalanchoe (which see).

TECOMARIA CAPENSIS CAPE HONEYSUCKLE

Scarlet Sprays and Glossy Foliage

A South African half-climbing evergreen with handsome, shining leaves and orange-scarlet flowers about 2 inches long. During the summer, these appear in dense clusters at the tips of branches. Though naturally a large shrub, it can be kept to 8- or 10-inch pots.

Cool greenhouse: 45° to 50°F.

Culture: Treat the same as Jasminum (which see)

TECOPHILAEA CYANOCROCUS CHILEAN CROCUS

Blue Beauty for Winter

A small, cormous plant from the Andes, easily forced into bloom by late winter. Flowers look like blue crocuses. They are an inch and a half long and appear on a single stem just above narrow, bright green leaves about 5 inches long. Fifty or more plants are needed to make a good display.

Cool greenhouse: 50°F.

Culture: Treat the same as Ornithogalum (which see).

Three Birds Flying (See LINARIA.)
Throatwort (See TRACHELIUM.)

THRYALLIS GLAUCA

Yellow Sprays and Blue-Green Leaves

A tropical shrub from Mexico and Central America with bright yellow flowers and long blue-green leaves. Flowers appear from late winter to early spring, when the plant is about 2 feet high. While this shrub can grow to 5 feet, it is possible to keep it for several years in an 8-inch pot.

Warm greenhouse: 60°F.

Propagation: By cuttings in a closed case at 70° in early spring.

Potting: Transfer rooted cuttings to 3- or 4-inch pots and shift to 5's or 6's before plants become pot bound. Transfer to 8-inch or larger pots when required. Top-dress or repot in February.

Culture: Use sandy soil with peatmoss. Feed every ten days during the growing season with liquid manure or a complete liquid fertilizer. Pinch off terminal shoots to induce bushiness, and grow in shade through spring and summer. Trim plants back hard after flowering to keep them shapely and under control. Maintain a high humidity and water freely through the summer, but moderately at other seasons.

Pests: Green fly, scale, and mealy bug.

TIBOUCHINA (PLEROMA OR LASIANDRA) GLORY BUSH

Months of Purple Bloom

A shrub or vine, fine for May-to-September bloom. This showy southern plant can be grown as a semi-climber 6 to 8 feet tall, or as a bushy, 3-to-6-foot pot plant. T. semidecandra (Pleroma macranthum or Lasiandra macrantha) is a vigorous vine with handsome, purple, cup-shaped flowers, up to 5 inches across (illustrated). They last but a day, but are at once replaced, and for nine months, plants are rarely out of bloom. T. elegans, a smaller plant, is also prolific with flowers one and a half inches across and of deeper hue. Both varieties bloom when quite small, that is, about five to seven months after spring cuttings are struck. Leaves are somewhat hairy and in maturity turn from green to red.

Moderate to warm greenhouse: 55° to 60°F.

Propagation: By cuttings. Those I begged were 3 to 4 inches long. Planted in March, they rooted in about 4 weeks in vermiculite. (I imagine they can be taken at other seasons and rooted, though perhaps less quickly later in the year, in sand, or sand and peatmoss).

Potting: Plant rooted cuttings in 3-inch pots of light fibrous loam with plenty of sand for free drainage. Transfer to 6's or 7's before young plants are pot bound. Shift to 10's for the third year. Top-dress or repot each fall.

Culture: Through fall and winter, give all possible sunshine. During late spring, shade partially from midday sun. In summer, set plants outdoors in a shady sheltered spot, such as the north side of heavy shrubbery. See that Tibouchina has all the water needed. It requires more, especially in the greenhouse, than most other potted plants.

Feed during the growing season every ten days with weak manure or with ammonium sulphate—1 teaspoon to 1 gallon of water—or use any complete liquid fertilizer you have found successful.

Pinch and prune both young and older plants, when they stop flowering, to produce shapely, side-branching specimens with plenty of flowering wood. Make the last pinch about mid-September, since flowers are produced on new wood. Remove weak basal shoots, and pinch back longer shoots as soon as they reach 2 to 3 feet. By the second year, specimen plants are at their best. Growth is slower and less pruning is needed. By the third year, potted plants will have passed their peak. New one-year plants should be kept coming along to replace them.

Pests: Red spider.

TRACHELIUM CAERULEUM THROATWORT

A Dark Blue-to-White Campanula

An herbaceous plant of the campanula family, native to the Mediterranean region. This beautiful plant, rather like Heliotrope, produces a terminal head about 6 inches across of deep blue to white flowers. It is summer-blooming, and grows to 3 feet, but can be held to 2 feet, if you prefer.

Cool greenhouse: 45° to 50°F.

Propagation: By cuttings in February, or seed sown in March at 60°. Rooted cuttings may be planted directly in 3-inch pots. Transplant seedlings to flats about 2 to 3 inches apart as soon as they are large enough to handle.

Potting: When young plants become well established, set fairly firm in 5- or 6-inch pots. Repot the following year in 7's or 8's.

Culture: This plant requires little attention beyond care in watering during the short days of fall and winter. Shade from the hot sun of spring and summer, but grow in full light the rest of the year. A rich soil, lightened with manure or peat-moss, is good. Feed every two weeks with manure water or a solution of ammonium sulphate—1 teaspoon to 1 gallon of water.

Pests: Aphids and green fly.

TRACHELOSPERMUM JASMINOIDES (RHYNCHOSPERMUM) — STAR OR CONFEDERATE JASMINE

Summer "Jasmine"

A semi-twining evergreen, native of China, recommended especially for beginners. It is of easy culture and does well even under crowded conditions. Fragrant white trusses occur at almost every joint. These open in rapid succession and keep the plant gay for several weeks in early spring; then there are flowers intermittently through the summer. You'll go a long way to find a better plant for small or large pots, or one that can be kept under control so easily. A yellow form is also available.

Cool greenhouse: 40° to 50°F.

Propagation: By cuttings from firm young shoots about 3 to 6 inches long. Take these in spring and root in a closed case at 65° to 70°. Several years are required to get a good-sized plant from a cutting, so it is advisable in March to order one or two that are well established.

Potting: Transfer cuttings to 3-inch pots, then to 6's or 7's. Young plants will make growth more quickly at 60° to 65°. The next year, top-dress or transfer to 9's or 10's, depending on size of root growth.

Culture: The soil for this plant should be light, loose, and fibrous so water will pass through readily. Lighten the soil with rotted manure, peatmoss, and sand, if it is heavy. Keep moderately moist at all times. Syringe every bright warm day and shade from burning sun from spring until fall. Pick off the first season's blooms to give strength to the plant. Train large specimen vines around bamboo stakes, or provide a light wire trellis 2 to 3 feet high. After flowering is over, trim into shape. During spring and summer, mature plants require feeding. Use ammonium sulphate—1 teaspoon to 1 gallon of water—or a complete liquid fertilizer. Pots may be plunged out-of-doors in summer.

Pests: Thrips, scale, mealy bug, red spider, and aphids.

TRICHOSPORUM PULCHRUM (AESCHYNANTHUS)

Scarlet Urns from Spring to Fall

A splendid flowering plant with thick glossy leaves for hanging baskets or pots. The beautiful curved tubular flowers, scarlet with yellow throats, are profuse in spring and continue to appear over a long period. The foliage, which is more compact than that of most basket plants, is attractive all year. Several baskets of Trichosporum suspended from the ridge will add a pleasing touch of atmosphere to any greenhouse. This location suits the plants very well, too, for they find the extra warmth near the roof most agreeable.

Warm greenhouse: 60° to 65°F.

Propagation: By cuttings of firm growth, 3 inches long, taken from March through summer. Root in a closed case at 80°.

Those a fellow gardener gave me made a mass of roots in ten days.

Potting: Transfer rooted cuttings to 3-inch pots; then on to 5-inch pots or hanging baskets before small pots become filled with roots. Set four or five plants to an 8-inch basket for a quick show. Transfer to 9's or 10's the following spring, depending on condition. When repotting, remove some of the old soil, but take care not to injure roots.

Culture: Good drainage is important. This plant needs lots of moisture during the growing season but cannot stand stagnant water at the roots. A fibrous soil that drains readily is essential to good results. Mine do well in a mixture of soil and dried sphagnum moss. This is definitely a warm greenhouse plant requiring 60° to 65° at night, and high humidity. Feed with ammonium sulphate or nitrate of soda—1 teaspoon to 1 gallon of water—every other week during spring and summer. Syringe daily, except when in bloom, and pinch the top growth of young plants two or three times during the first season. Do not allow the plant to flower until it has formed good growth. Shade lightly from spring to fall. Keep the soil on the dry side in early fall and winter. Plants flower on ripened growth so do not pinch the second season. Cut back after flowering to encourage more shoots and flowers for the following year.

Pests: Mealy bug and scale.

Tritonia (See Iris Family.)

TULBAGHIA

Year-round Lavender Loveliness

A small cousin of the agapanthus grown from a cormous rhizome. Flowers appear in attractive, starry, lavender clusters on 18-inch stems through most of the year. Evergreen, basal foliage grows up to about 10 inches and is pleasing, too. T. violacea (illustrated) has foliage which smells like garlic if bruised. T. fragrans, a larger species, has very fragrant blooms and odorless foliage.

Cool greenhouse: 45°F.

Propagation: By offsets taken when repotting, or seeds planted in February or March.

Potting: Use 5's, 6's or larger bulb pans depending on size of the display wanted. Set rhizomes about an inch apart and one-half inch deep. Repot when pan becomes overcrowded with roots.

Culture: Tulbaghia is of easy culture and flowered for me about a month after planting. Grow in sandy loam with a little peatmoss added. It requires plenty of water and two or three feedings after starting in growth. Use liquid manure, a complete liquid fertilizer, or nitrate of soda—1 teaspoon to

1 gallon of water. Grow in semi-shade during the summer and full sunshine the rest of the year.

Pests: None.

VALLOTA SPECIOSA (PURPUREA) — SCARBOROUGH LILY

Clusters of Scarlet Lilies

A South African amaryllid with spreading clusters of scarlet, lily-like flowers over 2 inches across. Being of easy culture, it is most desirable, but rare and often difficult to find. As with other amaryllids, it is impossible to say exactly when it will bloom, but flowers usually appear in spring or summer.

Cool to moderate greenhouse: 50° to 55°F.

Propagation: By offsets produced in large numbers. These are taken off after they have formed roots, at repotting time in spring or summer.

Potting: At every stage plant in as small a pot as possible. Smaller bulbs are planted in a 5- or 6-inch pot, while larger clumps may require an 8 or 10. Repot only when absolutely necessary, taking care not to break or disturb roots. It is better to leave the plant overcrowded in the pot since it is set back considerably if roots are broken. May to July is a good time to repot because this is the season when root action has just started and before flower stems have pushed up. I have never moved mine, since it takes several years to get a good specimen without repotting.

Culture: Vallota does well with little attention if perfect drainage is provided. Provide a rich soil, such as a mixture of equal parts sandy loam and decayed manure or peatmoss, with coarse sharp sand added if necessary. Some growers put one-half inch of coarse, gritty sand directly under the bulb to insure good drainage. Set the bulb in the soil with the nose slightly protruding. This is an evergreen plant and chances are there will be some leaves on the one you buy. Plenty of moisture is required when the plant is in growth, and the soil should be kept moderately moist even during the winter rest. Full sun is essential except during the hottest part of summer. Feed with a complete liquid fertilizer or liquid manure every two weeks during spring and summer. This is especially important with a mature plant that crowds the pot.

Pests: Snails and cut worms.

VELTHEIMIA VIRIDIFOLIA

Drooping Spikes of Showy Yellow

A bulbous plant from the Cape of Good Hope, bearing twenty-five to thirty drooping yellow blossoms tinged with red. The dense-clustered head is held on a stout stem. Wavy, sword-shaped leaves, 1 foot high, are shiny and attractive. If bulbs are started during November or December, they can be brought into bloom in early or late spring.

Cool greenhouse: 50°F.

Propagation: By offsets that will flower in two to three years. They are best separated when the bulb is dormant and has made several years growth.

Potting: Plant singly in pots 2 inches larger than the bulb. Repot or top-dress in August or September.

Culture: Veltheimia requires a loose fibrous soil with peatmoss, leafmold, or sand added as necessary to make it light and provide good drainage. Keep the soil fairly dry until growth appears, then soak thoroughly and continue to water well throughout the growing cycle. Feed with two or three applications of complete liquid fertilizer. Grow in full sun at 45° to 50°, for this plant will not stand hard forcing. After flowering, keep the plant growing in the sun. This is important, because it is during this period that it recovers strength to flower the following year. After leaves turn yellow and die back, let the soil dry off completely.

Pests: Aphids and red spider.

Veronica (See HEBE.)
Wand-Flower (See SPARAXIS.)
Watsonia (See IRIS FAMILY.)
Wax Flower (See HOYA.)
Yellow Flax (See REINWARDTIA.)
Zephyr Lily (See ZEPHYRANTHES.)

ZEPHYRANTHES ZEPHYR LILY

Something Different for Spring-to-Fall

A small bulb bearing large "lilies" in white, yellow, or red on thin bare stems, 6 to 12 inches long. Leaves are grassy and stay short until after the flower has appeared and then grow long. Though not often grown, the zephyr lily is a lot of fun and an interesting addition to the home greenhouse. It blooms in early spring, summer, or fall, depending on variety. The popular Z. candida is a late-flowering white species; Z. grandiflora (Z. carinata) the choicest midseason species, has large, rosy flowers up to 4 inches (illustrated); Z. insularum is an early white, lightly tinted pink. Z. citrina with bright yellow flowers is midseason. There are also many fine hybrids.

Cool greenhouse: 50°F.

Propagation: By offsets removed when the bulb is completely dormant. Bulbs will be damaged if separated in an active state. The strongest will flower the following spring.

Potting: Bulbs are small, an inch in diameter. Plant four or five to a 6-inch pot. Divide or repot in spring if the bulb pan is overcrowded and use a pot two or three sizes larger. Twelve or 14 bulbs planted in a 10-inch pot will flower in succession, a few at a time for several weeks.

Culture: Provide good loam and peatmoss in equal proportions. Water just enough to keep soil moderately moist. Grow in full sun except in summer, when partial shade is needed. After flowering is over, let the leaves mature fully. In the fall give just enough water to keep plants alive.

Pests: Aphids.

Index